JAMES McSh

The Spirituality of
Running

A Runner's Guide to
Physical and Spiritual Wellbeing

Published by Redemptorist Publications

Wolf's Lane, Chawton, Hampshire, GU34 3HQ, UK
Tel: +44 (0)1420 88222, Email: customercare@rpbooks.co.uk,
www.rpbooks.co.uk

A registered charity limited by guarantee
Registered in England 03261721

Copyright © Redemptorist Publications 2025
First published January 2025

Edited by Krista Nelson
Designed by Emma Repetti

ISBN 978-0-85231-645-0

A CIP catalogue record for this book is available from the British Library.

The publisher gratefully acknowledges permission to use the following
copyright material:

Excerpts from the New Revised Standard Version of the Bible: Anglicised
Edition, © 1989, 1995, Division of Christian Education of the National
Council of the Churches of Christ in the United States of America. Used
by permission. All rights reserved.

Every effort has been made to trace copyright holders and to obtain their
permission for the use of copyright material. The publisher apologises
for any errors or omissions and would be grateful for notification of any
corrections that should be incorporated in future reprints or editions of
this book.

Printed by Bishops Printers Ltd.,
Walton Rd, Drayton, Portsmouth PO6 1 TR

For Michael Munnelly,
a true friend, whose kindness and wisdom
have greatly enriched my life.

CONTENTS

First of all, a disclaimer: I'm neither a guru of spirituality nor a guru of running! What I am, I suspect, is someone just like you – someone who tries, and often struggles, to be spiritual and to run, but someone who understands the immense benefits both disciplines can have on one's life. We all know what running entails: simply putting one foot in front of another at a greater speed than walking. Being "spiritual" is harder to define: one can be spiritual in the traditional theistic sense (believing that God exists as a real entity), and one can be spiritual in the sense of, for instance, finding the spiritual in Nature, though not believing in the existence of a Supreme Being. Wherever one finds a sense of the spiritual, it's my firm belief that the simple act of running can enhance one's spiritual life, and one's spiritual life can enhance one's running.

Having acknowledged that a non-believer in the traditional theistic God can be spiritual, this book is primarily for those who do believe that God exists in a very real way: that he created the world in which we live and that he's concerned for us individually. My own faith tradition is Christianity, and much of the book will draw on the teachings of Jesus Christ, St Paul and other Christian thinkers, but I believe the book will be helpful to those of other faith traditions too: those of other faith traditions who put on their running shoes and run!

As human beings, we understand much of what we know by way of analogy or comparison: how often we say something "is like" or "it's as if" to help someone understand what we're trying to say. There are many comparisons between living a life that's spiritual and living a life that involves running: for instance, both require discipline and commitment if we're to benefit from either. I hope the analogies and comparisons between spirituality and running in the following pages won't become torturous – to me they've been a great means of helping me see that praying and running involve many complementary aspects and that these aspects combined can help us become spiritually and physically healthy individuals.

Like you, I have a body, and like you, I have a mind. Modern psychology demonstrates that our bodies and minds are integral: that the wellbeing of one is dependent on the wellbeing of the other. This isn't to say that as the body deteriorates with age a person deteriorates spiritually (on the contrary, old age and physical suffering can deepen a person's spiritual life), but it is to say that being physically and spiritually healthy is what we should try to be, for as long as we can be. In short, that's the aim of this book: to explore how we can harness our physical exercise, in the form of running, and our spiritual exercise, in the form of prayer, and by integrating the two, live as well as we can as the people we were created to be.

CHAPTER ONE
Just doing it!

Any Nike advert makes it sound so simple: "Just Do It!" This slogan is usually superimposed over an image of a toned athlete in a sprinting pose, sinews and muscles proof of countless hours of dedicated training. If only it were that simple. If only it was so easy to "Just Do It!" and look like the Olympian on the magazine page! Alas, most of us who run know how hard it is to even get to the front door, especially when the rain's falling and the temperature's hovering at the zero mark – or below!

And yet, if you run regularly, and in all weathers, you *are* disciplined. Nobody is forcing you to run – it's entirely your choice to get out there and run when it's cold or wet; you *choose* to endure the discomfort running brings. And you do this because you're disciplined. Those of us who run, however, know how easy it is to say, "I'll run tomorrow," or "I'll give it a miss today; one day off won't make a difference." But we know in our hearts that "tomorrow" will become "tomorrow" again the next time we're scheduled to run, and that "one day off" can so easily become many days off, to the point when you wonder if, in reality, you're really an *ex*-runner.

So, you know that running regularly requires self-discipline. Why? Because running is hard! Happy the man or woman who finds running easy! I speak as someone who's never experienced the "runner's high"; I speak as someone who's never been in that euphoric "zone", striding effortlessly along, breath and movement in perfect synch, mind elevated to a higher level. Yes, some runs are easier than others; some runs seem to require less effort, but for me, every run brings discomfort – no run is "easy". I take solace from Haile Gebrselassie, who said that "The first three miles of every run are very hard."[1] Imagine, Haile Gebrselassie, one of the greatest marathon runners of all time, finds a three-miler hard! If that doesn't make you feel better as you struggle for breath after five hundred yards, nothing will! When you watch a Gebrselassie or a Paula Radcliffe striding along at a five-minute-mile pace, it's easy to imagine that they're not really like the rest of us; that somehow they're superhuman and don't feel the pain we lesser mortals feel. Nothing could be further from the truth – if anything, they feel *more* pain, *more* discomfort. What athletes like Gebrselassie and Radcliffe have is iron determination and self-discipline on a scale few human beings ever achieve: that's what makes them great. Another professional athlete remarked that if you don't want to give up at least once on a run, you're not running hard enough! That's a sentiment I recognise, even when running "easy"!

So, you and I have a certain discipline; though, if you're like me, there are times when you struggle to make that morning run. Is it possible to turn yourself into that disciplined, never-miss-a-run man or woman? Can you *manufacture* that kind of determination? Yes, you can, but it takes practice! And the more you practise, the easier it becomes. Just as bad habits are easy to form, good habits can be formed too: what's required is consistency.

I imagine you're familiar with the following scenario. It's 6.30 a.m., and you become conscious of the bleeping alarm replacing that dream you've been having about something weird and wonderful; the duvet feels warm and comforting, and, though you placed your running kit on the chair by the bed last night in preparation, you really don't want to get up! Now you have to make a decision, a *choice* – either to stay where you are and drift back into delicious sleep or to get up, put your kit on, close the front door behind you and *run*. The more often you make the choice to run (and the choice not to turn over and go back to sleep), the more often you'll make the choice to run *in future*. In other words, the choice to run becomes easier; or, put another way, it becomes less difficult.

If we apply what I've written about running to prayer, the parallels are obvious: to benefit from prayer it has to be regular, it has to be consistent, and it requires discipline. If you re-read the previous paragraphs and substitute the word *prayer* for *running*, you'll recognise the sentiments as interchangeable. Almost!

Like running, prayer is a *choice* – nobody is forced to pray. The choice to pray stems from a desire to know God more intimately, to deepen the relationship we have with him. In the Christian tradition we know God as "Father", a term which implies relationship and intimacy. Although God is responsible for our existence, the term "Creator", sometimes used to describe God, can make him seem distant and detached, so we call him "Father". As human beings we know what it is to have parents, and we know what it is to have a relationship with our parents: we talk to them, we listen to them, we want to be in their presence, we want to tell them our worries and concerns, we want to share our joys with them. It's in prayer that we establish and maintain an intimate relationship with God our Father. As our Father, God desires that intimate relationship with us: he created us; he gave us life, and, therefore, we are his children. As his children we have a relationship with God, whether we like it or not. We can choose to ignore him, even pretend he doesn't exist, but he's our Father nonetheless. What parent doesn't desire regular contact with his or her children? What parent doesn't feel the sadness of being ignored by his or her child? If God is truly our Father, then it makes sense to have a relationship with him, and this relationship, like any relationship, is sustained and deepened through communication, which is simply what prayer is: talking and listening to God.

Do you remember your first adult run? I remember mine. After being very sporty as a child I hadn't run for fifteen years. Aged thirty-eight I decided to get fit, and so donned a pair of battered trainers, ran about two hundred yards and stopped, hands on knees, gasping for breath! That short run put me off running for two months. Then I tried again, this time with a friend. I didn't get much further than the previous two hundred yards, but this time I knew I'd persevere; two years later I ran my first marathon.

All runners who began running again after several years of inactivity will remember the suffering those first runs induced: the breathlessness, the pounding heart, the next morning's aching legs, the wanting to just stop and walk. And yet, they persevered and became *runners*. I persevered; *you* persevered. We share the bond that running creates between us. I may be overweight, you may be thin; I may run nine-minute miles, you may run twelve-minute miles; I may run marathons, you may run 5K's; I may run on the road, you may run on trails – none of this matters. What matters is that we both run, and we respect each other because we do. As we pass each other – running on the road, in the park, on a trail – the mutual nodding of heads is a gesture of solidarity; the briefly raised palm or the quietly spoken, "morning", is the recognition of fellow spirits. Whilst we're running, we're absolutely equal – you may work in high finance, earning a small fortune; I may work in a supermarket stacking shelves, earning just enough to get by, but when we're running our incomes don't matter. Running ensures parity: you're out of breath, I'm out of breath; your legs are tired, my legs are tired; you're feeling good this morning, I'm feeling good this morning; you're struggling on your third mile, I'm struggling on my third mile. Stripped of all but our running kit and shoes, we don't look very different, and our class, income and status aren't apparent: we're simply two people out running and glad of the support a fellow runner gives us as he or she runs by, gesturing softly, but meaningfully, in mutual recognition of a shared interest and pursuit.

Of course, just as our running renders us equals, so we're all equal before God: equal because, as our Father, he loves us without distinction or discrimination. What we do for a living, how much we earn, the house we live in, the car we drive, none of these things matters more than who we are and how we live.

Interestingly, our equality before God is never more apparent than in a church. I remember attending Mass at Westminster Cathedral in London. The lunch-hour congregation numbered about two hundred, consisting of white people, black people and Asian people, Chinese, Filipinos, Poles, Australians and other nationalities, among whom were bankers in pin-striped suits, shop workers, tradesmen, housewives, office workers and children, and it being central London, even men and women who clearly lived on the streets and were inside the cathedral just keeping warm.

Nobody was excluded; all were welcome. I can't think of many places where such a disparate group of people would sit side-by-side, would shake hands at the Sign of Peace and would acknowledge, in that sacred place, that the person standing beside them has, in God's eyes, the same value, esteem and worth as they have themselves.

Just as running liberates us from prejudice towards our fellow runners, so we're liberated from such prejudice when we stand collectively before God. He hears our prayers no matter what our backgrounds may be. He's with us in our joys and in our sadness, in our good times and in our bad times. In big races there are (quite rightly) "elite" runners, but to God there are no "elite" human beings: for him, there are only sons and daughters, all equally loved.

Knowing how much God loves us, why do we so often find prayer difficult? After all, it's only talking to a Father who cares deeply for us. Prayer is difficult for the same reasons running is difficult: it requires us to set aside time; it demands concentration; it means doing it when we'd rather do something else.

If running and praying are so often difficult pursuits, why should we bother practising either? The answer is, simply, that running brings us physical health, and praying brings us spiritual health. To be physically and spiritually healthy is to be at our best. If we run every day, we'll be in great physical shape; if we pray every day, we'll be in great spiritual shape, but if we *only* exercise, or if we *only* pray, somehow, we limp because one facet of our being is neglected: we're either neglecting our bodies or our spirits.

Of course, there'll quite possibly come a time in life when running, or any form of strenuous exercise, isn't possible: we'll age and our bodies may not be up to it. So, what should have priority, spiritual health or physical health? The answer must be *spiritual health*. I may be in fine physical condition, but if my spiritual life is poor (that is, I rarely, if ever, pray), I won't be truly happy (as St Augustine remarked, referring to God, "our hearts are restless until they rest in You"[2]). Conversely, I may be in poor physical health, but if my prayer life is good and I have an intimate relationship with God, I can be happy despite poor physical health. None of us will be at eighty the physical specimens we were at twenty: we can't defy age. However, we can be at our spiritual best at eighty even if our bodies are infirm or ill health has overtaken us. So, though spiritual health should take precedence over physical health, the ideal is to maintain both facets of our being in good order for as long as we are able. Why? Because what goes on in our minds can affect us physically, and what happens to our bodies can affect us psychologically.

For many centuries Christianity viewed the body as a malign influence on the mind or soul: a corrupting influence on our better, spiritual selves. The body caused us to be lustful; it caused us to be gluttonous; it led us into being sinful. Therefore, the body was seen as a hindrance to our spiritual development in that it interfered with our relationship with God. Sex was thought "dirty", if necessary, for procreation. But God gave us the bodies we have, and in Christian understanding, we are "Temples" of his "Holy Spirit". If God created and gave us the bodies our souls inhabit, then they are sacred, and if they are sacred, we have a duty to look after them.

Thankfully, a more optimistic understanding of the body has been recovered in Christian theology, and in the next chapter we'll explore just what it means to think of our bodies as "sacred" and the transformative effect this can have on our psychology and sense of self-worth.

CHAPTER TWO
We are sacred!

You may remember an event that took place in St Peter's Square at the Vatican in November 2013. Pope Francis, his weekly audience with the vast crowd almost over, was heading back to his apartments when he caught sight of a man in the crowd, a man whose face was extremely disfigured with numerous tumours. The Pope stopped the vehicle in which he was travelling and went to the man, embraced him for several moments and then kissed him on the forehead. In that moment, that man's life was transformed. At fifty-three years of age, Vinicio Riva, from Northern Italy, had been used to people recoiling at the sight of him. He recounted how people on buses would move if he sat next to them and how it was impossible for him to even think about entering a restaurant. All that changed with the Pope's embrace: within minutes videos of the encounter had gone viral, and what people saw on those videos was not a man with a hideous deformity but a human being made in the image of God.

That beautiful encounter between Pope Francis and Vinicio, as well as being intensely private, was also greatly instructive for the rest of us: their embrace speaks volumes to you, to me and to the world. Their embrace tells us that nobody is ugly; their embrace tells us that *everybody* is beautiful. And why is everybody beautiful? Simply because they've been made in God's image. Nothing made in God's image *can* be ugly.

But, you may say, some people are objectively more beautiful than others – how else do we explain Brad Pitt's almost universal appeal to women or Kylie Minogue's almost universal appeal to men? Yes, we instinctively know beauty when we see it, and we instinctively know that some people are more *physically* appealing than others, but what we are judging is a person's outward appearance. Why did the Pope stop and embrace Vinicio? He embraced him precisely because *superficially, outwardly*, he appeared hideous. But the Pope was saying to Vinicio, "What you appear to be on the outside is not what makes you the person you fully are; you have infinitely more worth and value than your physical appearance. How could it be otherwise – God made you, and nothing God makes is ugly. God made you; therefore, you are *beautiful!*" Imagine how transformative that message is; imagine how it feels when you become fully aware that you are beautiful! And you are beautiful, not because another human being looks at you and decrees that you are, but because *God made you*!

When God created us, he created us with a mind and a body: we are "embodied" people; we are "enfleshed". St Thomas Aquinas and St Augustine, both towering theologians of the Christian Church, rejected the notion of "Dualism", that is, the theory that the body and the soul are completely separate entities. Rather, they taught that the body and the soul are intimately related. I'm sure that when you think of yourself, you have an image in your mind of what you look like – I know I do. And how we perceive our physical appearance has a profound psychological effect on us. If we have a positive view of our physical selves, it can make a huge difference to our sense of happiness and wellbeing; conversely, a negative view of our physical selves can lead to deep unhappiness.

You and I are unfortunate in that we live at a time when what we may call "the cult of the beautiful" has never been stronger: an age in which being young and beautiful is seen as the pinnacle of human worth. Social media has greatly fanned the flames of this insidious narcissism to the extent that children take their own lives if their physical appearance is criticised on Facebook. Later in this chapter we'll look at how we can overcome a negative body image, but first it's important to understand *why* we may have a negative view of our physical selves.

Throughout history there have been those who've capitalised on human vanity, and it's easy to see why – we all like to look as good as we *can* look; we all like to enhance our appearance and make the most of ourselves. And this is no bad thing – it makes the world a brighter place;

it makes us feel better and, in primeval, Darwinian terms, it helps us to attract the opposite sex, find a mate, and propagate our species! So, vanity has a purpose and is distinct from narcissism. The enterprising exploit our vanity: they sell us clothes, they sell us cosmetics and they sell us diets. But most of all, they sell us dreams! If, they tell us, you wear this outfit, if you apply this or that cream, if you follow this diet, you'll be transformed: transfigured into a more beautiful self, a self others will admire and be attracted to. The dream, of course, has to be constantly changed and updated: clothes that are *in* today are *out* tomorrow; there's always a better, more effective "enhanced" or "improved" cream on the market; there's always a new diet to be followed. The appeal to vanity never stands still because the cash tills have to keep ringing!

But when does innocent vanity become self-centred narcissism? The line is crossed when the fashion industry goes beyond merely attempting to make us look good and begins to manipulate our sense of self-worth. I don't know if clothes designers, manufacturers of cosmetics and diet creators employ psychologists, but it's a fair bet they do!

Twenty years ago, if you bought a mobile phone, you bought it to make phone calls or to text friends and family. Now, all adverts for mobile phones concentrate on a built-in function: the camera! The selling point is that you'll be able to improve your selfies! You can take literally hundreds of photos, select and edit the one that's just right, delete the rest, then post on social media the ideal image you want the world to see! Young people strive to capture this perfect image of themselves, an image they'll present on Facebook, Instagram or the myriad of other platforms that cater for – and encourage – narcissism. The trouble is, there's no such thing as perfection, and the young now suffer an anxiety no previous generation was subject to – at least, not to anything like the same degree – the anxiety of trying to be physically perfect. This striving for unattainable physical perfection has inflicted huge damage on young lives: lives that should be carefree teenage years are now blighted by body-image anxiety, resulting in a surge in eating disorders, self-harm, mental health problems and even suicide. That the Internet and mobile phones are, in themselves, marvellous inventions is beyond question, but they're also inventions that, when misused, have led to a far less happy society and world. Of course, the Internet and mobile phones can't be *un*-invented; rather, we human beings need to use these resources properly: we have to learn to control *them*, and not let *them* control us.

What we need to find, in terms of our body image and in terms of what we physically are and look like, is *acceptance*: accepting that we're the people God created. Whether we are naturally thin or naturally big, whether we are objectively beautiful or objectively plain, whether we are disabled or non-disabled, whether we have flawless young skin or whether we have old, wrinkled skin, whether we attract admiring glances and compliments or whether we don't, our self-worth doesn't depend on what others think of us, or how they see us: it comes from being a son or daughter of the God who created us. If we really understand this, if we really take it to heart and believe it, a negative body image simply cannot be part of our thinking; rather, we can't help but have a positive body image simply because God cannot create, and has not created, anyone who's ugly or defective. *This is the absolute key to a life that's free from body-image anxiety.* I remember well a young girl of six named Lily at a school of which I was a governor. Lily had Down's syndrome. Before a Governors' meeting she said to a couple of us, "I'm beautiful!" One of the governors asked, "How do you know?" and she replied, "Because God made me!" If we all took heed of that six-year-old's insight and wisdom, we, and the world, would be so much happier!

I'm very fortunate to live in rural France, in an area called the Creuse, near Limoges. After pounding the streets of Essex and London for many years, it's a real joy to run in forests and beside lakes, both of which abound in this area. One of the drawbacks, however, is that almost every village, like mine, is overrun with cats. A week ago, two cats gave birth almost simultaneously in my barn, ten kittens in all. Sadly, eight of those kittens have died, and next to the desk on which I'm typing this manuscript is a box with a mother cat and the two remaining kittens. One of them is obviously struggling for life; the other seems to be doing well. If the stronger kitten lives, no doubt she'll become a part of the cat community here, a community which consists of five houses: the cats outnumber humans by four to one!

The last week has been a sad one, as each day I've wrapped at least one kitten in kitchen towel, placed the kitchen towel in foil and buried the kittens. Am I too soft-hearted, displaying a sentimentality for animals that have died and no longer exist? Shouldn't I have just put them in the rubbish sack with the household refuse and deposited them in the communal bin up the street? Maybe. But something told me that even the dead body of an animal should be treated with a certain respect.

Most of us have lost, or will lose, a loved one: those we love will die. This inevitability is part of life, and one day we'll die ourselves. A kitten's dead body can evoke a feeling of respect, but that respect is obviously minuscule compared to the respect we afford a human body that's died, especially to the body of someone we've loved. We know instinctively that this body isn't just a lump of expired flesh; that even though the heart no longer beats, the brain no longer functions, the blood no longer flows, this body has an innate dignity and deserves to be treated with reverence. The religious person may ascribe this sense of reverence to the body's once having housed the person's soul, or spirit; the non-religious may have a less explicable reason for this sense of reverence, but both have a real sense and understanding of the body's worth, and that that worth extends even when the body no longer has life.

Perhaps the greatest manifestation of this understanding of the body's innate value is the funeral service and burial. Family and friends come together in the presence of the body, now housed in a coffin or casket. When the service is over, the body is taken to its place of burial and interred with due solemnity, or, if cremated, the same solemnity will be afforded it at a later date. And long after the body is buried or cremated, loved ones will visit the grave, perhaps leaving flowers; they may spend some time at the graveside, simply remembering in silence the person whose life they shared. If our bodies are afforded such dignity and respect after we've died, shouldn't they be afforded the same dignity and respect whilst we're still alive?

The bodies we have are gifts from the God who made us, precious gifts that should be treasured and looked after as best we can. If I mistreat or abuse my body, I'm devaluing this gift and showing ingratitude towards the giver. So, we have a duty to treat our bodies well, to honour them as the gifts they are, and to be thankful to the one who bestowed them.

Acknowledging this, what does it actually mean to treat our bodies well? The first things that spring to mind when answering this question will probably be diet and exercise, and nutrition will form a part of the next chapter. But, if what we put into our bodies is of vital importance, what we *shouldn't* put into them is of equal importance.

Addictions to substances that are detrimental to our bodily wellbeing have risen exponentially in recent years, most notably Class A drugs. Drugs of the highest classification are now easily attainable – a mere phone call or text away. So many people now use drugs recreationally that any element of shame has gone, and society now tolerates drug-taking to the extent that many are calling for total legalisation. Drug users argue that smoking marijuana or snorting a line or two of cocaine at weekends helps them to relax, so where's the harm? The harm comes in two ways. Firstly, no illegal drug is beneficial to the body: quite the contrary, drugs are harmful to the body in so many ways, resulting in physical deterioration. Secondly, drugs are addictive and can lead to long-term abuse and very serious physical consequences. We know that the strength of marijuana has increased and has resulted in people suffering from long-term psychosis and schizophrenia – especially young people. Cocaine and heroin put great pressure on the heart in terms of a fast heart rate and speeded-up metabolism, and the body's general defence system has to work overtime to combat the effects of these drugs.

If we recognise our own bodies as sacred, as gifts from our Creator, we must, by extension, recognise the sacredness of others' bodies. This recognition then means treating *their* bodies with respect and not in any way using or abusing them. If a drug-dealer supplies substances that harm others' bodies, he or she is treating others merely as a source of revenue, totally ignoring another's sacredness; if I use another person's body solely as a means of sexual gratification, then I'm abusing that person physically (even if legally) and taking no account of that person's bodily worth; if I commit an act of violence on another's body without justification, I'm acting without consideration for that person's bodily dignity. These are examples of acting selfishly and *sinfully*. Acts which in any way denigrate or cause harm to another's body are also offences against the Creator who made that person, who gave them life.

St Paul uses a wonderful analogy when he compares the body and its parts to the Church, illustrating the connectedness and reliance we have to, and on, each other (1 Corinthians 12). He talks of the foot having its unique function, the hand having its unique function, and the eye and ear having unique functions. Each part of the body makes up the whole, and if one part of the body refuses to cooperate with the others, then the body doesn't function well. Although Paul used the analogy to highlight the cooperation necessary amongst Jesus' followers, the analogy can be applied to all of us: we rely on each other to perform our individual tasks in cooperation with others who perform their tasks, and this cooperation makes for a coherent and harmonious society. If I refuse to cooperate with other parts of the "body", then the "body" (i.e. society) suffers, becoming less coherent and less harmonious. By refusing to cooperate, as a member of the body, I'm actually damaging myself because I'm a part of that body, a body that, because of my non-cooperation, now suffers. The analogy illustrates how dependent we are on each other.

In the same chapter St Paul talks about each of us having different "gifts". God has given each of us a gift to be used for the good of all collectively. Some may have the gift of musicality, some a gift for medicine, some a gift for languages, some a gift for teaching, some a gift for simply listening, some a gift for running! All of these gifts, when "pooled", help to make a society that functions well. A mistake we make is in viewing some gifts as more worthy than others, and this is reflected certainly in the monetary value we place on them: hence a footballer is paid in a month what a nurse may take years to earn. We know that the pay of chief executives thirty years ago was twenty-five times that of an employee in the same company; today a CEO's pay is, on average, three hundred times more than an employee's. This distortion shouldn't distract us from a simple truth: God has given each of us something valuable, something we can contribute to society, and no gift has more or less worth than another. Having been entrusted with these gifts, we should try to use them as best we can.

The whole foundation of Christianity rests on the answer to this question: did Jesus rise from the dead, with his body intact, as he said he would? If he didn't, then Christianity joins a long list of spurious religions and cults. If he did, then Jesus is the Messiah, the Saviour, and his resurrection provides the rock-solid foundation for Christianity's truth. Many are said to have witnessed the risen Jesus, beginning with Mary Magdalene, who quickly informed Jesus' other disciples of her encounter with the Risen Lord. Soon these disciples would see Jesus for themselves, after which they would boldly go out and tell whoever would listen that Jesus was who he said he was, that he wasn't a deluded fraud, and that they'd had hard proof after seeing his physical self. Would those followers, knowing they faced certain death at the hands of the Roman authorities, have acted in this way if they weren't utterly convinced of the authenticity of Jesus' resurrection? Unless they had a collective death wish, or had entered into some strange mass suicide pact, it seems unlikely. Within a few centuries Christianity became the faith embraced by vast swathes of the world's population. Today, one third of the world's population still hold that belief, living their lives based on Jesus' teaching.

You, the reader, will have your own thoughts on the veracity of Christianity's claims about Jesus, and this book is not about trying to convert you to believe in him and the movement he began all those years ago. What is of the utmost interest, though, is the crucial aspect of Christianity's claim to truth: that Jesus rose from the dead *bodily*. Crucially, also, is the reason he did so – that his body wasn't just a mere casing for his soul, or something in which to house his spirit, but an integral part of who he was – his *body* and *soul* made up his persona: both elements of his being made him the person he was, physically and psychologically. His physical self contributed to his psychological self, and his psychological self contributed to his physical self. When Jesus returned to his Father, he ascended to heaven *bodily*, not as a manifestation of proof to those looking on, but because his body was part of his *person*.

What is true for Jesus is true for us: we are physical and we are psychological; we have a body and we have a mind, and these aspects of our being make us the people we are. If our bodies and minds are so intimately connected, what will happen to our minds (souls) and bodies after we die? Christian theology is quite clear that our bodies will be reunited with our souls, and both will live eternally. The Old and New Testaments refer to this reunification, perhaps most clearly in the letters of St Paul. When Jesus appeared to his disciples by the lakeside after he'd risen from the dead, at first they didn't recognise him because his body had been "transformed": clearly, in some way, his body was different. The Scriptures speak of his body as "glorified". What precisely this means is not possible to say. But the Christian believes that after death his or her body will also be "glorified". Again, this glorification is hard to define. We'll only know the full extent of this truth when we experience it, but we can speculate!

I remember a programme on the radio sometime in the 1990s on which various celebrities were asked the question, "What is heaven like?" Some said it was a place of peace, some said a place where we'll be with family and friends for eternity, and so on. If you think about it, nobody's actually come back from heaven to tell us, but we can speculate about what heaven *isn't* like based on passages from Scripture. Surely, we can say it *isn't* a place where cancer, heart disease or bodily pain exists; it isn't a place where there's hunger or poverty or wars; it isn't a place of heartbreak over broken relationships or separations; it isn't a place of infirmity or old age. Perhaps, positively, we can say heaven is a place where we'll be reunited with those we've loved and reunited with them for eternity; a place where we'll be happy and at peace for all time, without fear or worry; and a place where our bodies will be made whole, free from the pains and ailments we suffer here on earth.

In his Second Letter to Timothy, St Paul, perhaps nearing the end of his life, writes these words,

> *As for me, I am already being poured out as a libation, and the time of my departure has come. I have fought the good fight, I have finished*

the race, I have kept the faith. From now on there is reserved for me the crown of righteousness, which the Lord, the righteous judge, will give to me on that day, and not only to me but also to all who have longed for his appearing.
(2 Timothy 4:6-8)

St Paul uses beautifully the metaphor of running a race and completing it. His aim was to win the "crown of righteousness", which he did win because he "kept the faith". For those of us who run and try to live spiritually, those words of St Paul should be written on our hearts, and perhaps repeated as we stride along the road or the trail: we are running and living with a purpose, not just to enjoy physical fitness, but to win the crown of eternal life!

Because we run, you and I have a good idea of what we mean by "physical exercises": before we run, we may stretch, we may lift weights to supplement our running, we may do yoga or Pilates, or we may simply go for long walks – all exercise is good exercise.

For those who seek a close relationship with God, there are also exercises that have been practised throughout history, known as "spiritual exercises".

The words "exercises" and "practice" are the keys to living a spiritual life: they imply effort and routine. In this way, "spiritual" exercises are no different from "physical" exercises. To benefit physically from exercise, that exercise has to be regular; it has to be consistent. It may be something like:

Running: Monday, Wednesday, Friday and Sunday

Weights: Tuesday and Thursday

Yoga: Tuesday, Thursday and Saturday

Following such a regime would certainly exercise all parts of the body, and we'd be very fit if we did so! We may even define that regime more specifically by allotting definite times of the day to each exercise.

To benefit from our spiritual exercises, those exercises, too, have to be regular; they have to be consistent. They also have to be routine. You may prefer running in the morning, or you may prefer running in the evening, likewise with other forms of physical exercise. It's the same with spiritual exercises. The time of day physical or spiritual exercises are done isn't important; what's important is that we actually do them!

One of the great myths about modern living is that we struggle to "find time" in the day to do all we'd like to do. Yes, if you're a mother with two young children, your day will be quite full looking after them, along with fitting in all the other commitments you have. If you commute for an hour and a half to work and do the same commute to get home in the evening, that's a fair slice of the day eaten up with travelling. If you're looking after elderly parents, their needs will occupy a lot of your time. But, we're informed, the average person watches three hours of television a day and even more hours over the weekend. How many hours are wasted scrolling through mindless videos on the Internet or checking the latest opinions and comments on X (formerly known as Twitter)? If physical and spiritual exercises are important to us, we'll find the time to do them! It may mean getting up an hour earlier in the morning or setting aside an hour in the evening, but we can find the time if we really want to.

The key to "finding the time" is having a routine: to do our exercises *at the same time each day*, if possible. Routines become easier to follow the more they are practised. Usually, we start work each day at the same time – say, 9.00 a.m. – and we think nothing of it; we may go to a yoga class beginning at 7.00 p.m. on Wednesday evenings, and we're there on time, and again, we think nothing of it; we may meet friends for coffee on Saturday mornings at 10.00 a.m. and, unless there's a reason we can't make it, we *do* meet them. We follow routines because some routines are forced upon us, for example, our work commitments; others we follow because we *want* to follow them, as they bring us enjoyment. Routines benefit us, ensuring we don't drift aimlessly through life.

In the Christian tradition the most famous, and perhaps best known, spiritual exercises are those developed by St Ignatius of Loyola (d.1556), a Spanish priest and founder of the Jesuit religious order. His Exercises are divided into four parts (how long one spends over each part is for the individual to decide, perhaps with the guidance of a spiritual director). The four parts are Sin and God's Mercy, Episodes in the Life of Jesus, The Passion (suffering and death of Jesus), and the Resurrection of Jesus and contemplating the love God has for us. These Exercises usually take place over a thirty-day period and are best done with the help of a spiritual director. However, most people haven't the time to devote to Ignatius' Exercises, so in practical terms, which spiritual exercises can fit into an average day and deepen our relationship with God?

Times to pray

A practical routine for spiritual exercise, or prayer, is to divide the day into "prayer times": morning, midday, evening and night-time. In Chapter Five we'll go into more detail about ways to pray, but here we're laying down a structure for that daily prayer:

Morning

Thanking God for a new day and safe delivery through another night.

Asking God to help us through this day, especially if we have difficult tasks to perform.

Telling him about any cares or worries we may have and asking for his help with them.

Asking God's blessing on those we know who are ill or facing difficulties in their lives.

Asking his blessing on the world, especially on those countries suffering from wars, famine or disaster.

Commending those who have died to his care.

Spending a few moments thinking about all that's good in our lives – family, friends, health, the food we eat, the work we have – and giving God thanks for his generosity in giving us these joys.

Dedicating ourselves today to God's service and the service of those who may need us.

Midday

Reading a passage from the New Testament (or from other holy scriptures, if one is not of the Christian faith) and spending ten to fifteen minutes thinking about what God may be saying to us through this passage and how the passage's message may apply to us.

Evening

Thanking God for the day thus far.

Thinking about what's gone right today and what may have gone wrong.

Commending to God anyone we may have encountered today who's in need.

Asking him to bless anyone we've met today who's made us happy and to bless anyone we've had disagreements with, trying to see them not as enemies but as God's sons or daughters.

Reiterating our gratitude for all the good things God has given us and asking his guidance through the coming evening.

Night-time

Conducting an Examination of Conscience – looking back over the day and asking what went well and what may have gone badly. For example:

- Was I kind or unkind towards people?

- Was I patient with those who tested my patience?

- Was I generous with my time for those who needed me?

- Did I do my best at work?

- Did I resist or succumb to anything that called on me to make a moral or ethical decision?

Thanking God for the day that's nearly over.

Making a resolution to live as well as we can tomorrow.

Asking God to grant us a restful and peaceful night's sleep.

Of course, you may wish to adapt the above schema to suit you. It's a prayer routine I've used for many years, and I've always found it tremendously helpful, in good times and in bad. The morning prayer takes about twenty minutes; the evening prayer the same; midday reading and reflection, fifteen minutes; and night-time prayer, twenty minutes: approximately an hour and fifteen minutes in all.

The place where one prays should be a quiet place, free, if possible, from distractions. In Chapter Five we'll look at aids to prayer, in the sense of icons, candles, the Crucifix and so on.

Types of prayer

The three elements that make up the prayer routine outlined above are: thanksgiving, petitionary prayer and reflection.

Thanksgiving

When we offer thanks to God, we're automatically reminded of the many good things we have in life: family and friends, food and drink, a place in which to live, employment, good health, the beauty of Nature, and the fact that today we can run! The good things we take for granted are given a new perspective: we now see them as gifts from a God who cares for us. We may be going through a rough time, perhaps suffering from a bereavement or a broken relationship; we may be living in poverty; we may have an addiction to alcohol, drugs or gambling; we may be in poor health – we may, at times, feel as though we haven't much to be thankful for. But even when we undergo hard times, we can express our gratitude to God for the good things we *do have*, and this does lighten our burdens. We know God is with us; we know he cares for us; we know we're not alone in our suffering.

Petitionary prayer

Petitionary prayer is simply asking God for what we need and for the needs of those for whom we pray. Jesus assures us that if we ask, we shall receive (Matthew 7:7). We may have needs for today or needs for the future, but whatever those needs, we place them in God's hands. An important part of petitionary prayer is that we're acknowledging our dependence on God: without him, neither we nor the world in which we live would exist. We're also expressing our trust in a Father who wants what's best for us. It can be disheartening when we feel our prayers aren't answered, as they so often seem to be. At these times we have to go on trusting, trying to understand that God sees a much bigger picture than we can see. Perhaps what we're asking for isn't right for us at that moment; perhaps he has another plan for us, a plan we'll come to realise is the right one for us. When we place before God our needs, we're implicitly placing our trust in him, and we're acknowledging his power to grant those needs. After making known to him our needs and the needs of those we pray for, we leave them in his hands, trusting in his goodness and concern for us.

Reflection

At no other time in our history have there been so many distractions, distractions which have greatly reduced our capacity for self-reflection. The mobile phone is the greatest distraction of all: we can text, play games, watch videos, be immersed in the "Twittersphere", and much more besides. Hardly anyone in a train carriage or on a bus will be gazing into space, absorbed in private thought; rather, they'll be staring at a screen, fingers busy scrolling up and down. Does this matter?

Socrates, the Greek philosopher, believed that "an unexamined life is a life not worth living". How would he view the way we live today in this age of technology and social media? It's a fair bet he'd be dismayed at our diminishing capacity for self-reflection and self-awareness. His view was that without self-examination we are no higher as a species than animals; without self-examination we become creatures that eat, sleep and procreate, nothing more. What raises us above animals is our ability to reason and to understand who we are and what we were created for.

Human beings have always asked existential questions, questions such as: Why am I here? Who, or what, made me? What is my purpose in life? What happens to me when I die? These questions can only be answered through reflection, reflection that brings self-awareness. Through self-awareness we come to understand the meaning of our existence, our place in the world and our relationship with our fellow human beings. *Not* to understand the reasons we exist, or our place in the world, or our relationship with others, is to be deeply impoverished. Are we losing the capacity to ask these existential questions? And, if the questions aren't asked, then obviously we will never find the answers. Perhaps it's too early to tell, but what is clear is that the mobile phone, despite all its capacity for good, is harming our ability to think. George Orwell, that most prescient of political commentators, talked in his book *Nineteen Eighty-Four* about the state constantly monitoring people through means of a "telescreen": telescreens were ubiquitous in homes, in the workplace, in places of entertainment, in the streets: nobody was free, even for a second, from their all-seeing gaze. Perhaps Orwell had it only half right: yes, the screens are constantly watching us, but we're also constantly watching the screens!

I remember an interview on TV with Paul McCartney in which he was reflecting on his childhood in Liverpool. One wet, dull Sunday afternoon he was staring out of the window, bored. Boredom led him to pick up his guitar and he wrote the song, "I'll Follow the Sun", one of the most beautiful Beatles songs. He was aged fifteen. Would McCartney have written that song had he had a mobile phone? The chances are, instead of reaching for a guitar, he'd have reached for the phone! Boredom has been a huge force for good throughout the centuries, prompting people to create music, art, literature and poetry. Movements that have benefited humankind may have been the result of somebody having an inspiring idea – possibly because they were bored. Had they been occupied on social media, the idea may never have arisen.

Another aspect of a God-given capacity that's in danger of being lost because of social media and the Internet is our capacity to imagine. If our minds are "captured" by a never-ending stream of video clips, the imagination is "turned-off", unable to freely wander where it will. Imagination can inspire thought, and thought can lead to action, action that leads to changes for the betterment of societies. Martin Luther King Jr's great "I Have a Dream" speech, though seemingly ad-libbed, must have been the result of him quietly thinking – imagining – what the world would be like if those dreams he mentions in the following excerpt became reality.

I have a dream that one day this nation will rise up and live out the true meaning of its creed: "We hold these truths to be self-evident; that all men are created equal".

I have a dream that one day on the red hills of Georgia the sons of former slaves and the sons of former slave owners will be able to sit together at the table of brotherhood.

I have a dream that one day even the state of Mississippi, a state sweltering with the heat of injustice, sweltering with the heat of oppression, will be transformed into an oasis of freedom and justice.

I have a dream that my four little children will one day live in a nation where they will not be judged by the color of their skin but by the content of their character.

I have a dream today.

I have a dream that one day down in Alabama, with its vicious racists, with its governor having his lips dripping with the words of interposition and nullification, one day right down in Alabama little Black boys and Black girls will be able to join hands with little white boys and white girls as sisters and brothers.

I have a dream today.

I have a dream that one day every valley shall be exalted, every hill and mountain shall be made low, the rough places will be made plain, and the crooked places will be made straight, and the glory of the Lord shall be revealed, and all flesh shall see it together.[3]

That famous speech, the fruit of Martin Luther King Jr's imagining, shaped the future of the United States of America, proving, beyond doubt, that the imagination, if it's allowed to roam freely, has the power to change the course of history.

Reflection, then, is a vital aspect of what it is to be a human being and something we all need to engage in if we are to understand ourselves and our purpose in the world. Daily reflection helps us know where we are in life. It helps us know how we're progressing, highlighting the areas where we're doing well and the areas where we're not doing well; it helps us understand those aspects of our lives we need to change. Reflection, as part of daily prayer, means we're reflecting on our lives in light of the relationship we have with God. God becomes the reference point for how we view our actions day to day and helps us determine whether we're following his will or not, and, if we're not, affords us the opportunity to change and live the way we were created to live. This is the goal of self-reflection: to live in conformity with God's will.

Living "in conformity with God's will" can be difficult in an age when so many people pay little heed even to God's existence. Søren Kierkegaard, a Danish philosopher and theologian, outlined three stages of moral development a person may pass through before conforming wholeheartedly to God's will. The first stage he called the "aesthetical". In this stage an individual lives solely for his own pleasure, for example, by picking up and ditching sexual partners, regardless of their feelings. The second stage he called the "ethical", the stage when the individual begins to take life seriously and commits himself to perhaps his family or a good cause. The third stage Kierkegaard called the "religious", the stage whereby the individual realises that only with reference to God does his life have meaning: only a belief in God can make sense of life and the world. The individual then puts himself under God's authority and acts morally, not just because it's conventional to act that way, or the Law demands that he does, but because God wants us to act that way.[4]

This has implications for us today, perhaps more than ever. Most people live at the ethical stage, committed to families, doing useful work and so on: they're good and useful members of society. But once we've entered the religious stage, we've placed ourselves under God's authority and we act accordingly. Reaching the religious stage isn't possible without self-examination, which requires us to reflect on our lives on a regular basis and adapt them to God's will. To live in the religious stage is to be *complete*, to be *whole*, to be close to God our Father. Yes, we can be happy living in the ethical stage, leading good and useful lives, but, as St Augustine says, "our hearts [will be] restless". Only living truly under God's authority and conforming to his will, will we find the deep joy we crave.

CHAPTER THREE
We are what we eat!

Even in this age of TV dinners and microwaved food, we all understand the great significance food and drink play in our lives. Whenever we want to mark an occasion, we do it gathered around a table, upon which will be good things to eat and drink. A wedding reception is almost unthinkable without the bride and groom, their families and guests, eating and drinking, whether it be in an upmarket hotel or in a simple community hall. Reunions of those who've shared some task or interest in the past usually take place over a meal. When friends want to get together, often a restaurant is the place they'll meet.

Food is functional, in that it keeps us alive, and symbolic, in that it symbolises friendship. Science may one day present us with a pill that will contain all our daily requirements of vitamins and minerals (think of the advantages: more time to do those household chores!). But imagine going to a party, a wedding reception or a reunion of old friends and there's no food or drink – the symbolism of the food and drink would be missing, and, one suspects, the events wouldn't quite be the successful occasions organisers and guests hoped they would be!

Every faith tradition understands the importance food plays in their rituals and worship. In the Christian tradition we believe Jesus, on the night before he died, gathered his disciples around a table for a meal we know as the "Last Supper". The food Jesus and those disciples shared symbolised the friendship between them. Jesus wanted those disciples to remember him, and not just those particular disciples, but all his followers for the rest of time. But how should they remember him? By coming together to share a meal. "Do this", Jesus said, "in memory of me." For over two thousand years Christians have remembered Jesus in this way: coming together to share bread and wine, the bread and wine symbolising his body and blood

– the body and blood he sacrificed out of love for us. For some Christians the bread and wine *symbolise* his body and blood; for others they *become* his body and blood. Whatever view one holds theologically on this point, all Christians share the belief that Jesus intended us to remember him within the setting of a meal.

As people, we understand the importance food plays in our lives – we know it keeps us alive, and we know its importance for sustaining our friendships. As runners, we know these things too, but we also know the importance of eating the *right* food: food that will nourish our bodies and help them cope with the stresses and strains physical exercise puts on them.

To be physically healthy, we need the right nutrition; to be spiritually healthy, we also need the right "nutrition". What we put into our bodies and into our minds makes a huge difference to how we are physically and mentally. If we eat healthily, we'll feel so much better physically; if we "feed" our minds healthily, we'll feel so much better mentally.

To live healthily – physically and mentally – requires living a healthy "lifestyle". We hear so much these days about "lifestyle choices", and perhaps that phrase is apt for what we're trying to achieve as runners and spiritual people. To achieve both requires a certain mindset, a state of mind that says, "I am a runner and I am a pray-er. *This is what I am;* this is how I live my life!" It would be good to remind ourselves of this regularly, repeating those words as a mantra – perhaps before we run or before we pray – as a first step to committing to this lifestyle. Those two words, *runner* and *pray-er*, will help define who we are and sustain us in the exercise of both.

When we make a serious commitment, we take an oath, or we make a vow: we do this when we get married, we do it when we're ordained for ministry in a church, we do it when we commit to serve our country. Vowing to ourselves to be physically and spiritually healthy is a serious commitment: a commitment that will change our lives for the better.

The way to achieve this lifestyle is obvious – we feed our bodies healthily, and we feed our minds healthily.

All governments now spend huge amounts of money instructing us on how to live and eat healthily, even to the point of insisting that each dish on a menu is accompanied by the number of calories we'll consume if we order it. Yet most of us know what healthy food is, and we know what unhealthy food is. We know that eating fruit and vegetables is healthy. We know that consuming too much sugar is unhealthy. We know that too much salt or processed meat in our diet is detrimental to our health. We know all this, yet we have an epidemic of diabetes in the Western world and a growing diabetes problem in developing nations. The explanation for this is simple: food loaded with sugar and salt tastes good! How else do we explain the ubiquity of McDonald's, Kentucky Fried Chicken and the countless other "fast food" outlets that dominate our high streets? People aren't stupid – they know it's healthier to cook and eat a vegetable lasagne at home than it is to have a Big Mac, and yet, if health statistics are to be believed, so many choose the Big Mac more often than they choose the vegetable lasagne! Having said that, there's nothing wrong with having a Big Mac, or some fried chicken, or a Coke or a large slice of cake – nothing wrong at all – if these foodstuffs are occasional and don't form the bulk of our diets.

I suffer from coeliac disease, which is an intolerance of gluten. Gluten is found naturally in wheat, but it's also used as a bulking agent in many foodstuffs. This means I have to avoid bread, cake, biscuits and all foods made from wheat, but I also have to be careful not to consume foods where gluten is "hidden", which are numerous, for example, brown sauce. Of course, this can have an impact on one's social life, for instance, when eating in restaurants or at friends' houses. The temptation may be to "give in" on those social occasions and eat the bread in the restaurant or the delicious-looking tiramisu at a friend's house. When coeliac disease is first diagnosed, it's very hard to resist temptation, and one learns the hard way from the resulting bloating of the stomach and the pain that goes with that bloating. However, over time temptation becomes easier to resist, to the point where living without glutenous foods becomes a *lifestyle*.

A *lifestyle* is precisely what a runner and a spiritual person should try to adopt. What exactly is a "runner's lifestyle"? And what exactly is a "spiritual lifestyle"? The answers to these questions may seem obvious: runners run and spiritual people pray – but there's more to it than that!

Underpinning the lifestyle of the runner and the person who prays is a psychology and an identity. As a coeliac, I have to *think* like a coeliac, and I have to *be* a coeliac. As runners, we have to *think* like runners and *be* runners, and as spiritual people, we have to *think* like spiritual people and *be* spiritual people. In other words, we aren't just runners on Mondays, Wednesdays and Saturdays; rather, we're runners even when we're not running. Similarly, we aren't just spiritual people when we pray in the morning and evening; we're spiritual people even when we're not praying! Achieving this state of being requires a certain psychological shift and an adoption of an identity. Once we've attained this identity, the way we think and the way we act follow naturally: the way we see ourselves, how we treat others, our attitudes to what's happening in the world and our relationship with God are all now lived from the perspective of this identity.

St Augustine coined the phrase, "we are what we eat". In Catholic theology the bread and wine, which are consecrated during the Mass, become Jesus' actual body and blood. Augustine was saying that regular participation in the Mass and the consuming of Jesus' body and blood makes us more Christ-like in the way we think and in the way we act. For this reason, he said, "If you receive [Jesus' body and blood] well, you are yourselves what you receive."[5] Whether one holds the view that the bread and wine become Jesus' actual body and blood (transubstantiation) or not, when we participate together in worship and share bread and wine in Holy Communion, we're strengthened to live the way Jesus taught us to live: to be compassionate, to have consideration for those less well-off than ourselves, to have a care for people who are elderly or disabled and to treat all people as brothers and sisters, irrespective of their colour or creed.

If we are what we eat, what we eat is of the utmost importance. And what we *don't* eat is of great importance also. In the same way, what we feed our minds will have an impact on us spiritually.

We all know what constitutes "junk" food, food that might taste good whilst we're eating it but has little, if any, nutritional value. After we've eaten this type of food we often feel worse than we did before it reached our stomachs. A common reaction may be, "I wish I hadn't eaten that," followed by a resolution to avoid junk food in the future. Junk food, or fast food, may be convenient, it may save us the time we would have spent cooking healthier food, but if we consume too much of it on a regular basis, over time our bodies will suffer: we'll put on weight, our arteries will become clogged and we'll be at greater risk of suffering heart attacks and strokes. Junk food, occasionally consumed, isn't going to kill us, but, as runners, we have an added incentive to avoid it most of the time. If we want to run well and benefit from running, we have to eat healthily: it makes no sense to run, say, thirty miles a week and subsist on hamburgers and ice cream! Eating healthily is a part of the lifestyle we should adopt as runners. The chances are, if you run regularly, you *do* eat healthily. The more we run regularly, the less tempting junk food becomes, precisely because we recognise the contradiction between consuming foods high in fats and sugar and the physical effort we put into running to remain in good physical shape. We also know that the benefits we gain from running, in terms of a healthy heart, lower blood pressure, reduced cholesterol and so on, will be negated by eating unhealthily.

The right nutrition, then, is crucial if our bodies are to be healthy, but also for our sense of wellbeing. If we eat moderately and eat a balanced diet of fruit, vegetables, fish, seeds, unprocessed meats, and oils high in omega-3, -6 and -9, then we just *feel* better! If we eat junk food, we can feel sluggish and often bloated. Our bodies are highly complex and sensitive organisms, and they have no trouble letting us know if we're feeding them with good food or bad!

If, as runners, we try to avoid junk food, similarly, as people who value our spiritual lives, we should try our best to avoid a junk lifestyle. Like junk food, a junk lifestyle may afford us temporary pleasure, but eventually it becomes corrosive and demoralising.

The world today offers us many opportunities to lead junk lives, with certainly the Internet and social media allowing us access to as much junk as we can handle. Pornography, dubious "dating sites", the negative aspects of Facebook, Instagram and X, all can lead us to places where we shouldn't go, and they can consume so much of our time.

As junk food is nutritionally empty, so junk time spent on the Internet is spiritually empty. The Internet, however, is now a fact of life, and it isn't going to disappear. As people who wish to live spiritually, we have to approach the Internet with caution, utilising the wonderful opportunities for knowledge it affords us but using it in a morally responsible way. Countless surveys have indicated that too much time spent online increases levels of stress and anxiety, and stress and anxiety are manifested through unhealthy bodily responses. Both anxiety and stress prompt the body to produce adrenaline and cortisol, flooding the bloodstream with an overdose of these hormones, which further increases levels of stress and anxiety. These hormones are very useful in certain situations, for instance, if we're under attack and need to react quickly to avoid danger. However, if these hormones are introduced into our systems unnecessarily, without the need to avoid danger, they can lead to rapid heart rate, breathlessness and high blood pressure.

Anyone who's suffered, or suffers, from panic attacks will know the terror they can induce: the pounding heart; the feeling of absolute dread, even the absolute conviction that a heart attack, stroke or death is imminent. And no matter how many times panic attacks happen, it doesn't seem possible to be rational about them: the sufferer doesn't say to him- or herself, "Well, I've been through this many times; it'll all be over in an hour or so." No, each attack is unique, and the sufferer doesn't have the capacity to rationalise them away. The bodily system is flooded with adrenaline and cortisol, which exacerbate the sense of panic. If adrenaline and cortisol are expelled from the body's system, that sense of panic is reduced. There are two ways that greatly help eliminate these hormones from the bloodstream: exercising and praying.

The classic way to reintroduce a sense of calm during a panic attack is to breathe deeply and slowly. If we want to eliminate these toxic hormones *quickly*, running is a very effective way to do so. These hormones are introduced into our system to help us fight or flee, and when we run, we're doing exactly what they're intended to help us do. So, when we run, we're working *with* adrenaline and cortisol, not fighting against them, and the physical effort involved drains them naturally from our systems. The added psychological benefit of running *during* a panic attack (or doing any form of physical exercise) is that we can say to ourselves afterwards, "I've just increased my heart rate to a high level and put my body under physical strain, and I'm still alive – nothing bad happened to me!" This reassurance is invaluable in restoring a sense of calm. The worst thing we can do when having a severe panic attack is to do nothing – to do nothing except lie or sit there suffering wave after wave of dread.

Whilst running during a panic attack, we can pray. We can put our anxiety in God's hands, asking him to reduce our fear. When the attack is over, we can give him thanks for helping us shoulder our burden of panic and ask his help in our struggle with such a debilitating condition.

I'm able to humbly offer that advice because, for many years, I suffered severe panic attacks and still do occasionally. I learned that it was useless to lie there passively, allowing the panic to overwhelm me. I also learned that two or three large glasses of red wine is only a temporary fix: once the effects of alcohol have worn off, the panic may indeed worsen. I now know that exercise and prayer will greatly reduce the severity of panic attacks, and it's a knowledge I'm hugely thankful to have.

All of us have relationships with other people; those people may be family members, friends or work colleagues. These relationships will, on the whole, be good relationships, relationships that help us lead happy, fulfilled lives. We may also have relationships which are less positive: relationships that sap our sense of wellbeing, that make us unhappy, that impact negatively on our spiritual lives. But, for some reason, we continue these relationships and don't have the courage to end them.

Relationships of this kind drain us: they provide us with nothing good or wholesome, nothing that nourishes us intellectually or emotionally. We continue these relationships because we feel a sense of obligation to those with whom we're involved; we may feel guilty if we were to end them. Cutting someone out of your life, perhaps after many years, is difficult, even if you know you'd be better off if you did sever the relationship.

Relationships are meant to be two-way, a giving and a receiving. But what if it's you who does all the giving? What if it's you who never receives anything in return?

I was once on the upper deck of a London bus; two women were in the seat in front of me. One of the women said, "My mother's been diagnosed with breast cancer," the other woman immediately replied, "My mother had breast cancer..." and went on to describe in great detail what she and her family had gone through. I could see the look of dismay on the first woman's face. She'd revealed, perhaps *confided*, to her friend something of huge importance to her – *her mother has breast cancer* – and yet, for all intents and purposes, her friend hadn't heard what she'd said: hadn't *heard* in the sense of understanding her friend's need to share something of great concern. Instead, she'd turned the conversation and topic back to herself. My guess is the second woman, like so many people, *never* listens to what others are saying. We all know people like that. We know that an encounter with them won't be a shared conversation; it'll be just us listening to what they want to say. Is it worthwhile continuing such a relationship? A relationship we come away from feeling dispirited and undervalued, as if our opinions and thoughts aren't worth listening to? Could we class this sort of relationship as "junk"? Is this a relationship we'd miss? Is it one we'd be better off without?

Similarly, we may ask those questions about those we know who are constantly negative in their talk, their views and their attitudes to life in general. Nobody can be upbeat and positive all the time, and we wouldn't expect them to be, but someone who's relentless in their negativity can have a negative impact on us too. Just as healthy food nourishes us and keeps our bodies healthy, so healthy relationships keep our minds and spirits healthy.

Relationships, as we know, can be complicated, involving all kinds of dynamics and psychological dependence. We know some people endure abusive relationships for years, and we ask why – why doesn't the abused person end the relationship? We know some relationships between parents and children, or between siblings, are abusive and manipulative and, being familial, these relationships are hard to abandon. Those who can't free themselves from such negative relationships aren't to be judged in any way harshly; in fact, not judged in any way at all – nobody knows the psychological pressures or circumstances that keep those abused people in such relationships. But for those who have negative relationships that aren't familial, how is it possible to end them, or at least, avoid them as much as possible? Firstly, there has to be an acknowledgement that these relationships are not in our best interests. Secondly, there has to be a willingness and determination to act: to do what is necessary to sever ties with whoever is having a negative effect on our lives. The courage to do this shouldn't be underestimated, but the resulting benefits are so very worthwhile. To be free of such relationships is to gain spiritual health.

To live, we must eat, and the type of food we eat is entirely up to us. We can choose good, wholesome, healthy food, or we can choose junk food. How we live our lives is, again, entirely up to us: we can choose healthy relationships, we can choose to participate in activities that lift our spirits, we can be involved with organisations or charities that help others. Or we can choose to be in unhealthy relationships and be involved in activities that are soul-destroying, diminishing our capacity for joy. God has given us free will; how we use that free will is our decision. Moral theologians speak of a "fundamental option" – this term was coined in the 1970s by theologians living and working in countries such as El Salvador, Argentina, Brazil. The "fundamental option" called for a decision on whether one was on the side of the poor and oppressed or whether one was on the side of the oppressors, notably the military juntas that ruled South American countries at that time.

That term, "fundamental option", can be usefully adopted by us today: we can apply it to any situation in which we have to make a moral decision. Each of us has a God-given conscience: we know what's right and we know what's wrong.

To take two examples. Number one: you're in the gym's changing rooms, and you notice a wallet or purse in an open locker. The changing rooms are empty, and it would be the easiest thing in the world to remove the exposed bank notes and slip them into your pocket. Nobody will ever know.

Number two: you're at a party without your partner, husband or wife, and the man or woman you find very attractive is paying you a lot of attention, finally asking for your phone number and suggesting you meet sometime soon.

Both scenarios demand you make that fundamental option: to steal the money or not to steal it, or to hand over your phone number, knowing it could lead to an affair and a betrayal of your partner, or to politely refuse to hand over your number. In each situation, you may be tempted, so the fundamental option may also involve resisting or giving in to that temptation.

"Detoxing" is something we're all now aware of: a process which can last just a day, a month or longer. The idea of detoxing is to rid the body of impurities. This may mean detoxing from alcohol, from drugs or from eating too much unhealthy food. Detoxing may be a good idea, but only a good idea if we're not going to put these toxins back into our bodies in future. Without a firm resolution not to do so, and the discipline to sustain that resolution, detoxing is a waste of time. If we *can* sustain that resolve, then the initial detox has been a success.

A detox may mean literally ridding our systems of unhealthy toxins, or it may be metaphorical in the sense of ridding our lives of unhealthy activities, habits, pursuits and people. The metaphorical detox is likely to be the harder of the two to accomplish, especially "detoxing" from the people who affect us negatively. A good idea is to make a list of the things, and yes, the people, we would prefer not to have as part of our lives. Once the list has been made, we have to resolve to act on it, asking God's help to sustain us in our determination.

Once free of these negative impacts, we have room and time to replace them with more positive influences. Perhaps we've decided to avoid most social media, giving us more time to read interesting literature. Maybe we're resolved to eat healthier food, allowing us to rediscover the joy of cooking. It may be we've decided that some people we have a relationship with are no good for us spiritually or emotionally, so we've made a decision not to see them in future, freeing us to cultivate relationships with people who'll have a positive impact on our lives. It could be, if we're heavy drinkers – to the point where drinking is having a detrimental impact on us and our relationships – that we seek help with our drinking problem. It could be using our time more effectively, turning the time we waste into time used positively, perhaps by becoming involved with a charity.

Those involved in the Alcoholics Anonymous programme maintain that one cannot free oneself from addiction to alcohol without the help of a "higher power". This "higher power" is left to the individual alcoholic to determine what, or who, precisely, that higher power is. The point is that the person can't overcome his or her addiction alone: in most cases sheer willpower isn't enough – the help of something, or someone, "greater than ourselves" is required. To rid ourselves of a junk lifestyle, we also need the assistance of a "higher power". For most of us this higher power will be what we know as "God" in the traditional theistic sense.

Junk food is hard to give up, as is a junk lifestyle. We can try to reject a junk lifestyle solely through willpower, but chances are we'll fail. We may succeed for a while, but without God's help we may well relapse, finding ourselves reliving the bad habits of the past, and thus further demoralising us as we feel a sense of guilt and failure.

Prayer is the most effective way to help us jettison negative parts of our lives, those parts of our lives we want to be rid of. We need God's help, and we have to ask for that help. With his help a new future is possible, a future free from all that's making us unhappy. A better future may require effort and, at times, having to make difficult decisions, but we weren't created to be unhappy. God created us to lead happy and fulfilled lives and, if we allow him to help us, that happiness and fulfilment can be ours.

CHAPTER FOUR
Diets and dieting

Diets, like fashions, come and go, maybe because that's precisely what they are: fashionable. The likelihood is, at some stage in our lives, we've followed at least one diet. We can almost chronicle our lives from the times different diets were popular – though none of us was around in the 1830s when diets began to emerge as ways for losing weight! You may recognise several from the following:

1963 saw the introduction of Weight Watchers.

In 1971 we had the Grapefruit Diet.

1975 saw many in the USA following the Cookie Diet.

Slimfast was launched in 1997.

The 1980s dietary trends included the Cabbage Soup Diet.

The Atkins Diet emerged in 2003, closely followed by the South Beach Diet.

In 2007 it was the Raw Food Diet.

"Juicing" became the way to lose weight in 2010.

In 2016, Gwyneth Paltrow made popular the Goop Diet.

We could add to these the Apple Vinegar Diet, the F-Plan Diet, the Special K Diet and many more.

How is it that none of these diets have had long-term success? How is it that one diet trend follows inexorably after another? The answer is very simple: *diets don't work!* If even one diet did work and was proven to work long term, it would be the diet we'd all be following! Yes, you may lose weight in the short term, but inevitably, that weight will be regained. In the meantime, the inventors of these diets are happily banking your money and living very nicely on the proceeds!

What is the psychology of those who diet, for, surely, there must be one? People aren't so naive as to believe that this or that diet will be the one that helps them reduce weight and keep that weight off over a lifetime. So why do people in their millions go out and buy the book, then the ingredients, and follow a regime they know they'll only adhere to for a few months before moving on to yet another diet?

Perhaps the answer to that question can be illustrated by way of an analogy. "Retail therapy" is a phrase we're all familiar with. Shopping and buying items makes us feel good – we literally have a release of endorphins when we make the purchase, bring it home, try it on or put it on display. Unfortunately, the "therapy" is short-lived: a few days later we need more "therapy", and off we go to the shopping mall to repeat the process.

Diets are no different. It may be that the diet is intentionally short term, perhaps to help us fit into that swimsuit we're planning to wear on the beach. Maybe the diet is because we've been invited to a wedding and we want to look as good as possible at the reception and in the photographs. In this, diets may achieve their purpose – short-term weight loss – but diets, followed for a short time, have a similar effect on us to retail therapy: they make us feel good, but like retail therapy, the feel-good factor doesn't last long. It quickly fades when the weight starts to go back on.

Of course, there are those who swear by a certain diet and stick to it religiously. This prompts a further question: is a "particular" diet, maintained over many years, healthy? "Diet" implies eating certain foodstuffs and *not* eating others. If we take the "gluten-free diet" as an example, those who follow such a diet will avoid wheat, not to mention other foodstuffs where gluten is introduced as an ingredient. But if you're not a coeliac – someone allergic to gluten – why would you want to cut out wheat from your diet when wheat is a perfectly healthy food to consume? Diets *prescribe* certain foods and they *proscribe* certain others. Such hard-and-fast rules, where eating is concerned, can't be healthy.

The word "diet" implies a time limit, something temporary. You may ask, "But what about a Mediterranean diet? People in Southern Europe eat such a diet all the time." That's precisely the point: the food they eat isn't a *diet* in the sense that it's planned and lasts for a certain, limited time – it's simply what Southern Europeans eat! I had the good fortune to live in Italy for two years, and the food I ate there was very healthy: pasta, vegetables, fruit, extra-virgin olive oil, hardly any processed meat and never, apart from Sundays and feast days, desserts. The Italians don't follow a diet; they just eat what they've always eaten, which happens to be highly nutritious, healthy food!

I read in a magazine that the average woman spends thirty-five years of her life "on a diet" – half a lifetime! (Some wag suggested the other half was spent eating chocolate! Statistics for men's beer drinking weren't given!) How these figures are arrived at, who knows? If that statistic is accurate, though, it proves beyond doubt the popularity of diets, and it also proves, beyond doubt, their ineffectiveness. If diets don't work, what then is the answer to maintaining a healthy weight? The answer is a simple equation: calories in, calories out! If we consume more calories than we expend, we'll gain weight; if we expend the calories we consume, we'll maintain a healthy weight; to lose weight, we have to expend more calories than we consume.

We can circumvent the need to diet by simply eating healthily. Eating healthy foods, low in "bad" fats and sugar, will help us maintain a healthy weight. If we're overweight, we're simply eating the wrong foods and, probably, too much of them! The diet industry is huge, ranging from the seriously scientific, producing any number of academic studies, to the weight-loss classes in church halls. That such an industry exists is proof that too many of us are eating unhealthy foods and consuming these foods in vast quantities.

Is there such a thing as a "runner's diet"? Yes and no. As with any activity it all depends on how many calories running consumes. To maintain a healthy weight, someone who works on a building site will probably need to consume more calories than someone who works in an office, the builder expending more calories than the office worker. The runner who runs sixty miles a week will need to consume more calories than the runner who runs twenty miles a week – again, to maintain a healthy weight. If you run ten miles at a moderate pace, you'll probably expend a thousand calories; if you run five miles at the same pace, you'll probably expend five hundred calories. But this isn't to say there's a *runner's diet*, in the sense of following a regime of what to eat and what not to eat: it's simply a question of eating healthily and eating more if calorie expenditure exceeds intake due to running.

As with the person who goes on a temporary diet to fit into a swimsuit or attend a wedding, so runners will from time to time go on a temporary diet. The difference is runners are trying to *increase* their calorie consumption, not reduce it. To run any distance of more than a half-marathon (13.1 miles or 21.1 kilometres), muscles – especially leg muscles – need to be supplied with the right nutrients, notably carbohydrates, if they're not to run out of "fuel" over such long distances. When this "fuel" runs out, the muscles fill with lactic acid, causing pain and muscle seizure. Hence runners will "carbo-load" for a few days before a marathon or a half-marathon. When these runs have been completed, a normal eating regime is resumed. Unless you're someone who runs over forty miles a week, a "normal eating regime" should suffice in meeting your dietary requirements.

In the previous chapter we talked about rejecting a junk lifestyle, and it will be helpful to examine what may be called a "spiritual diet". As with a food diet, a spiritual diet isn't about the short term; rather, it's simply about feeding our minds with content that nourishes them. As with food, there's good intellectual content and there's bad intellectual content. Each of us should look at what we're consuming intellectually and ask ourselves if that content is spiritually uplifting or spiritually corrosive. We could ask this question in terms of what we watch on TV, what we view on the Internet, which magazines we read, which people we associate with. We could also ask if this content brings us closer to God or distances us from him.

Just as healthy food shouldn't be viewed in terms of "a diet", but rather simply "the way we eat", so leading a healthy spiritual life is simply a way of *being* – being the people we were created to be: God's sons and daughters. The secret to maintaining this way of being is prayer, and we now turn to that subject in the following chapter.

CHAPTER FIVE
Many ways to run, many ways to pray

If you're anything like I am, you'll love making plans as far as running is concerned. There's nothing like finding a comfortable chair and, diary and pen in hand, writing out that 10K or half-marathon running plan. Also, if you're anything like I am, you'll love reading running magazines or books about running, even though the magazines and books say virtually the same things in every edition! Then there are the running shops – brand-new running shoes, running shirts and shorts, running jackets for winter and summer, gloves, socks, gadgets ... the list goes on! Between planning, reading and looking, it's easy to think of oneself as a runner – without actually running! We can kid ourselves only so far, but we know eventually there comes a time when we have to actually put the plan into practice, use the knowledge we've gleaned from the magazines and books, put on the running gear we've so admired – and run!

All of us, as runners, are individuals, and as individuals we all have likes and dislikes when it comes to running. Some of us love to run long distances; some of us love short runs. Some of us love to run cross-country, while others prefer to run on urban streets. Some of us like to vary the distances we run; some of us like to run the same distance every time. Some of us like to enter races, but some of us wouldn't dream of doing so. There's no *wrong* way to run – there's only the right way, and the right way is *your* way.

As with running, so with praying: there's no *right* way to pray; the only way is *your* way. But, as runners and pray-ers, our ways of running and praying can be enhanced by using tried and tested methods runners and pray-ers have utilised for centuries. These methods aren't mere variations to stop us from becoming bored with our prayer life or running regime; rather, they're methods that bring us closer to God and improve our levels of fitness. It may be that you try these ways of praying and running and find one or two that suit you, affording you the opportunity to incorporate them into your daily prayer or running. The important thing is to use and adapt the methods that work for you. Firstly, we'll look at different ways of praying.

If you find yourself in a bookshop and scan the shelves marked "Spirituality" or "Religion", you'll find scores of books on prayer and how to pray. So many, in fact, that praying can seem like a science, and if it's a science, it must, therefore, be difficult! Praying can seem a mystery, such a mystery that only those who study and practise this art for many years appear to have any chance of acquiring the desired proficiency. Nothing could be further from the truth. Praying is simple! When we talk to someone, we don't theorise about the concept of "talking"; we simply say what's on our minds. And when we listen to someone talking, we don't theorise about the art of listening; we simply hear what they say. Prayer is simply talking to and listening to God. Yes, there are different ways to talk and listen (ways we'll now explore), but, in essence, that is what prayer is – *there is no mystery*! It's similar with running. We can study all the theories relating to physique, muscle structure, lactic acid, when to rest, different ways to run, and so much more, and yet, running is simply putting one foot in front of another at a pace faster than walking. Theories and guides on prayer and running are important, but praying and running are both very simple activities, and we shouldn't be put off doing either because theories make them appear complicated.

When we pray, we can use "set" prayers, prayers we read in prayer books or recite from memory. Other set prayers include the Rosary, the Lord's Prayer or passages from Scripture, including the Psalms. Our bodies need to be kept hydrated, so drinking water throughout the day is important. It's also important for us to be kept spiritually hydrated, and set prayers can help us be just that. We may be driving or in a queue at the supermarket, and we can use these times to pray set prayers, perhaps for a special intention. We can pray set prayers as we run. Thus, set prayers, uttered throughout the day, hydrate us spiritually and keep us close to God.

If we're praying at home, *where* we pray is important. If you share a house with others, then it will obviously be more difficult to find a quiet space for prayer. If this is the case, it may be worthwhile praying before others in the house are up and about or after they've gone to bed. Perhaps it may be best to find a church and pray there when the church is quiet.

If you *can* find a quiet space at home, you may wish to use aids to help you focus on your prayer. Candles can help foster a calm atmosphere. Incense can induce a tangible sensory mood and symbolise our prayers rising to God, the way incense has been used throughout the centuries. Christians can have on display a Crucifix or an icon of Jesus placed on a table, a visual image which helps focus our gaze and thoughts. A Bible, or other holy scriptures, can be displayed with an open page, symbolising God's Word, a word he may wish to speak to you during your prayer time. You may like to have soft, gentle music playing quietly, music such as Gregorian chant or other ambient music. All these aids help us know that the time spent in prayer is special time, sacred time, the time we give to God and the time he gives to us.

Ways of praying

In a previous chapter we outlined a schema for prayer in the morning, at midday, in the evening and at night-time. That schema laid down a structure for set prayer and, I know, from personal experience, how beneficial that way of praying is. The following ways of praying you may find valuable to use during those set times or at other times. Later, we'll examine the benefits of mixing up different ways of running, but first we'll look at the different ways of praying we can use to enhance our spiritual life.

Mantra

A very good way to begin praying is by using a "mantra", a word or phrase spoken softly, out loud or internally, and repeated over and over. A mantra can also be repeated at any time during the day. One can have a "personal mantra", a mantra one uses all the time, or different mantras as the occasion suits. A personal mantra could be, "Lord, help me love others as you love me." Mantras for different occasions could be based on Scripture, such as, "Come to me, and I will give you rest"; "Lord, have mercy on me, a sinner"; or "I am the Way, the Truth and the Life." Mantras, because of their repetitive nature, induce in us a sense of calm and are very helpful in preparing us for prayer, though they are actually prayers in themselves. Mantras, I've found, are very helpful when one can't fall asleep as they help calm the mind and distract us from the thoughts keeping us awake, and, again, they are prayers, so we're praying as we go to sleep. Prayers such as the Rosary could be described as "extended mantras": the repetition of Our Fathers, Hail Marys and Glory Be's also induce a state of calm, and the Rosary is a wonderful way of praying when we're tired and words aren't easy to find.

Imaginative prayer

One of the greatest gifts God has given us is our ability to imagine. Imagination is unlimited: we can literally imagine anything, and we can utilise our imaginations positively as part of our prayer life.

St Ignatius of Loyola, the founder of the Jesuit religious order, recommended as an aid to prayer that when we read a passage from the Gospels, we actually put ourselves into the scene, imagining ourselves to be one of the characters. For example, in the parable of the "Prodigal Son" (Luke 15:11-32), we could imagine ourselves to be either the younger or elder brother. By identifying directly with one of the characters, we gain a greater insight into the Gospel message and how this message relates to us personally.

Here's another example of a passage that could be used, this time from St Matthew's Gospel:

As [Jesus] walked by the Sea of Galilee, he saw two brothers, Simon, who is called Peter, and Andrew his brother, casting a net into the lake – for they were fishermen. And he said to them, "Follow me, and I will make you fish for people." Immediately they left their nets and followed him.

As he went from there, he saw two other brothers, James son of Zebedee and his brother John, in the boat with their father Zebedee, mending their nets, and he called them. Immediately they left the boat and their father, and followed him.

    (4:18-22)

Firstly, imagine the scene: the Sea of Galilee; it's a hot day, but the heat is tempered by a cooling breeze. Fishermen are unloading great quantities of big fish, and there's much banter being exchanged between them. It's a lively, busy atmosphere. Now imagine you're Simon Peter. You're mending your nets after a fishing trip, your haul safely stowed and ready to be taken to the marketplace. A man is approaching and he says to you and your brother, "Follow me, and I will make you fish for people." You have no hesitation in leaving your nets and following him.

Reflecting on the scene, now ask yourself the following:

What does this man, Jesus, look like?

Why is he calling me, a humble fisherman?

What is it about him that makes me leave everything I know and follow him?

What does he mean when he says, "I will make you fish for people"?

Then, returning to the present, and leaving the Gospel scene, you might ask yourself:

How is Jesus calling me?

What purpose, or path, is he asking me to follow?

Can I be like Simon Peter and put my total trust in Jesus?

Am I prepared to follow him, no matter the cost?

After reflecting on these questions, you could finish with a prayer, such as:

Jesus, you have called me for a definite purpose. Help me to be like Simon Peter; help me to place my total trust in you and follow you without hesitation. Amen.

Contemplative prayer

Our world today is a busy world! We can watch TV around the clock; the Internet and mobile phones keep us "connected" to the point where we're never fully switched off; we can even go shopping in the middle of the night!

As an antidote to this 24/7 existence, many people have turned to practices such as "mindfulness" to alleviate the stress and anxiety such constant activity induces. Mindfulness is a type of meditation by which you focus on being intensely aware of what you're sensing and feeling. Practising mindfulness involves breathing methods and other practices to relax the body and mind and help reduce stress.

Contemplative prayer has similarities to mindfulness, but its main objective is to simply be in God's presence. Psalm 46 tells us to "Be still, and know that I am God." In this form of prayer, no words are necessary – we simply place ourselves in God's presence and experience the peace and joy being in God's presence brings.

A great help to "being still" is silence. Silence, for so many of us, is difficult to find, but finding a place – a place free from distractions – where we can be as silent as possible is important.

You may wish to light a candle and burn some incense. If you can adopt a posture whereby you kneel with your bottom resting on your heels, you may find this helpful, or you may just sit in a comfortable chair. Begin by breathing in and out slowly. After a few minutes, allow your mind to let go of thoughts. If thoughts come to mind, don't fight them; just try to let them go. Focus on God's presence, a presence that's very close to you. Try not to worry about time. You may then wish to repeat a phrase, as in using a mantra, such as, "My Lord and my God, you are close to me." After repeating the phrase, return to emptying your mind of any thought, allowing yourself once more to rest in God's presence.

Coming to the end of this prayer time, finish with a prayer, such as:

Father in heaven, I thank you for your presence; I thank you for the time we've spent together. May your presence stay with me always, and may I always feel the joy of being close to you. Amen.

Many who run speak of a "runner's high", a feeling of euphoria as they stride along. Contemplative prayer often induces in the person praying a "pray-er's high": a feeling of deep joy and peacefulness. Spending time in the presence of someone you love, and who loves you, doesn't have to involve speech or any other form of communication: their presence is simply enough to induce in you a real sense of joy. Spending time with God in contemplative prayer can bring us this joy in abundance.

Prayer of praise and thanksgiving

You may recall the story in St Luke's Gospel of the ten lepers who were cleansed by Jesus (17:11-19). Though they had the faith to believe Jesus could heal them and were overjoyed when they were freed from such an awful disease, only one leper came back to thank Jesus. From the passage we can see that Jesus is disappointed by their ingratitude.

How easy it is for us to take what we have for granted, to give no thought or thanks to the provider of such gifts. When we praise and thank God for all we've been given, it makes us aware of the blessings we've received and reminds us of how fortunate we are in so many ways.

Saying thanks doesn't cost us much, but it means a great deal to the one who's thanked. Sending a card to thank a friend for a dinner party they've given is a small thing in itself, but it makes a statement to the receiver: that their friendship and generosity are valued and appreciated.

Praising God for his goodness towards us and thanking him for all he's given us should be a part of our daily prayer. Not to thank him is to be like the lepers who never returned to Jesus: they were aware of what he'd done for them, but hadn't the grace or manners to say thank you. As our Father, God is like any parent: we are his children, and like any parent, he likes to be thanked and appreciated for what he's given to us or done for us.

Prayer of confession

All of us, at times, do the wrong thing, the thing we know we shouldn't do, the thing that offends God. Traditionally we've called such things *sin*. We instinctively know when we've sinned because of our God-given conscience. As giving thanks to God is important, so is saying sorry for the things we've done wrong. Expressing sorrow is a part of a healing process. If we've offended someone and we neglect to say sorry, the relationship can remain strained. If we do say sorry, the relationship has the possibility of being healed. When we say sorry, it gives the person we've offended the opportunity to forgive, and forgiveness is another part of the healing process.

When we sin, we distance ourselves from God, even subconsciously, and, the greater the sin, the greater that distance can be. Expressing our sorrow before God is the beginning of an end to any rift between God and ourselves. Asking God's forgiveness, and being forgiven, completes the process of healing. No sin is beyond God's forgiveness, and his forgiveness is there if we ask for it, always.

Often, if we've offended someone, we may present them with flowers, a box of chocolates or some other gift. Our sorrow and desire to be forgiven are expressed symbolically in the gift. If we've sinned, we may want to express our sorrow to God in a similar, concrete way. We may go without a meal; we may donate money to a charity; or we may go out of our way to help someone in need.

At the end of each day, as mentioned in Chapter 2, an *Examination of Conscience* should be part of our prayer. If during that day we've done something wrong, we should ask God's forgiveness and his help in avoiding repeating that something in future. Reminding ourselves in this way of our sins helps us acknowledge them and strengthens us to avoid them in the days, months and years ahead. God wants nothing more than that you "return to [him] with all your heart" (Joel 2:12). The Prayer of confession allows us to do just that.

Ways of running

From the moment a child can stand upright, he or she wants to run. As young children, we run without any thought as to *why* we're running: we simply love the feeling running brings. It may be that something of the survival instinct is at play: at some stage in the future, running may save our lives, so the earlier we learn how to run, the better. Running, then, comes naturally to the human species, and it's a pity that as people get older, they run so much less, if at all.

You and I are fortunate that running still plays an important part in our lives. The chances of us having to run in order to escape with our lives will be very rare, if ever, so we run, not out of necessity, but mainly for health and fitness. Wouldn't it make sense, then, to optimise the benefits we gain from running? The simplest way to do that is to vary the ways we run. Mixing up runs increases speed, stamina and strength. Another benefit of varying runs is that it keeps us interested: we're not just repeating the same run five times a week, which can become monotonous. So, what are the various ways of running we can use to optimise fitness?

Base run

A base run is the run you'll do most often during the week, say, two or three times, and should be run at a comfortable pace. It may be that your base run is three miles or six miles, whatever distance is right for you.

Long runs

Long runs should be runs we do at the end of the week after the other runs have been completed. The aim of the long run is to build endurance, and they should be run, like a base run, at a comfortable pace. If you're aiming to run a half or full marathon, long runs are absolutely essential. To run a half-marathon, you'll need to be able to run eleven miles without being too discomforted; to run a full marathon, you'll need to be able to run twenty-two miles without serious difficulty. I always try to do my long runs on Sundays, Sunday being the day I can spare the extra time needed to complete the long runs.

Fartlek runs

Fartlek is a Swedish word, meaning "speed play". Incorporated into a base run, fartlek running is putting on bursts of speed for short distances, perhaps two to four hundred yards, and then resuming base run pace. How often you put on these bursts of speed is up to you, as is the speed itself, but it should range from faster than the base run pace to an all-out sprint. What works best for me is to run two-thirds of my base run distance and incorporate sprints into the run. However, there are no hard-and-fast rules, and you'll doubtless find what's best for you through experience.

Tempo runs

A tempo run is a run that could be described as harder than a base run but not so hard that you're struggling for air. If you plan to run a half or full marathon, tempo runs are highly recommended as they increase your lactate threshold – in other words, as lactic acid is produced in your muscles, especially the legs, the body is able to eliminate it at the same rate, thus avoiding what's known as "the wall", which is the point at which the legs become saturated with lactic acid and they seize up, rendering the runner unable to run further without great difficulty.

Interval runs

Interval runs are run at a fast pace for, say, four hundred yards before resuming a base-run pace. During these runs a set number of intervals is prescribed. Interval runs increase speed and endurance. These runs should be run once a week after a runner is comfortable with running two or three base runs a week.

Hills

Running hill repetitions isn't easy! The good news is that they build real strength and are over in a relatively short time. Again, hill repetitions should only be done when a runner has a good base level of fitness. All you have to do is find a steep hill and run up it, then jog slowly back down and repeat the exercise. How many repetitions one does is up to the individual runner, but they shouldn't be done to the point of exhaustion.

Recovery runs

Recovery runs are meant to be just that: recovery! They're used to keep the legs ticking over, as it were, and they should be run at a slower pace than even a base run. A heart-rate monitor can be useful in measuring your effort: if, for instance, your heart rate during a base run is 140 beats per minute, a recovery-run heart rate might be 110 beats per minute.

You will have your own schedule for running. Mine, more often than not, looks like this:

Sunday: Long run

Monday: Recovery run

Tuesday: Base run

Wednesday: Fartlek run

Thursday: Tempo run

Friday: Hill repetitions

Saturday: Rest day

The following week I'll exchange the fartlek run for an interval run. On the third week, I'll substitute hill repetitions for an extra base run. On the fourth week I'll rest on the Saturday and Sunday.

Of course, if you're planning to run a half or full marathon, you'll need to adapt the schedule to accommodate these longer runs. There are many excellent training schedules to help the runner prepare for these endurance events. (You may notice I haven't used the word "races", even though they are *races*. That's because, for me, when I've run half or full marathons, I haven't been *racing* against others – I'm happy just to improve my times, and even happier to complete another long, demanding run!)

We are one body

St Paul states that as Christians we belong to the "body of Christ": "Now you are the body of Christ and individually members of it" (1 Corinthians 12:27). If this is so, there can't be such a thing as an "isolated Christian": by our very nature as Christians, we're connected to each other, and this connectedness is most apparent when we come together to worship God, or for any activity to which our common faith draws us. This can be in a church, a house, or a place where we've gathered with the intention of carrying out, for instance, a charitable action. Yes, we can pray alone; we can praise and thank God alone – as we do most of the time – but Jesus didn't mean for us to do this *all of the time*. We were given the Sabbath day to come together and worship God collectively.

When we join together with other Christians, our faith is bolstered and supported, and this can be vitally important when we face difficult times. Also, our capacity for charitable works as Christians is hugely increased when we act collectively. Christians make up a third of the world's population, affording us immense power to do good, as is demonstrated in so many ways on so many occasions. Only fifteen per cent of the world's population are atheists or agnostics, and other faiths such as Judaism, Islam, Hinduism and Buddhism also contribute greatly to alleviating poverty, sickness and deprivation of all kinds. Of course, atheists and agnostics are good people, and they too are responsible for so much good being done for those in most need.

Recent decades have seen a rise in what may be termed "individualism". Individualism is the idea that each person should think and act independently rather than depending on others or the state. It has a long history in terms of philosophical and socio-economic theory and politics, but individualism has come to the fore very prominently in the USA and Western Europe since the 1980s, notably through the influence of Margaret Thatcher and Ronald Reagan. Mrs Thatcher is reputed to have stated, "There is no such thing as society, only the individual", though whether she did is disputed. "Collectivism", on the other hand, is a philosophy that emphasises the needs of the group, or community, over unrestricted personal freedom and individualism. Collectivism, in the communist sense, espoused by Russia and China, may be seen as the polar opposite of individualism, but the Chinese and Russian collectivist states are perversions of the collectivist idea and certainly do not operate for the benefit of the many over the few.

Is individualism, then, inimical to Christianity? The answer must be yes, as Christians belong to the same body – namely, Christ's. St Paul tells us that each member of the body of Christ has been given a gift (1 Corinthians 12:7-10), and these gifts are to be shared for the good of the whole. After Jesus ascended to heaven, his early followers shared everything in common: "Now the whole group of those who believed were of one heart and soul, and no one claimed private ownership of any possessions, but everything they owned was held in common" (Acts 4:32). These passages demonstrate the collectivist nature of Christianity and a rejection of an individualism that seems to be gaining ever more ground in Western societies.

Christianity, like other faiths, is a huge force for good in the world, but only a huge force for good if Christians act more collectively than individually – the individual Christian can achieve relatively little on his or her own.

Though we belong collectively to Christ's body, for the most part our prayer life will be solitary, talking and listening to God alone. This, in practical terms, is how it should be. Jesus himself instructs us on how to pray when he said to his followers:

> But whenever you pray, go into your room and shut the door and pray to your Father who is in secret; and your Father who sees in secret will reward you.
> (Matthew 6:6)

Mark's Gospel records Jesus praying in solitude:

> In the morning, while it was still very dark, he got up and went out to a deserted place, and there he prayed.
> (Mark 1:35)

Though Jesus prayed alone, he worshipped, along with others, in the Temple:

> When I was with you day after day in the temple...
> (Luke 22:53)

Ideally, then, our prayer life should be collective and personal.

If praying – and the rewards we gain from praying – is optimised by praying with others and praying alone, what of running? Is it best to run with others or to make running a solitary pursuit? This will largely depend on the temperament of the individual runner. As with praying, most of our runs will be run alone (or with a friend, but not in a large group). There are advantages to both running as a group and running by oneself, as we shall see.

Running with others

On the whole, shared experiences are the best experiences. Gazing at a stunning sunset whilst sitting on a sandy beach can be greatly appreciated by a solitary viewer, but the experience is somehow enhanced if he or she has someone to share it with. I've run marathons, alone and with others, and I can say, without question, the ones I ran with others were the more enjoyable.

The enjoyment from running marathons with others wasn't just about the marathons themselves or the shared sense of achievement on finishing them. The enjoyment was also there in the months of preparation: those early morning runs in the rain and cold (the London marathon takes place in April, hence the freezing January and February runs!); those long weekend runs of sixteen, seventeen, nineteen, twenty, twenty-two miles; and the inevitable setbacks when you, or your running partner, has an injury. And, on the day, the journey to the marathon itself, and then the shared nervous excitement as, along with thousands of others, you edge to the start-line. Then off to run twenty-six miles, confident you can finish, because you know you've done the training: those hundreds of miles you've run in all weathers with the person running beside you. And afterwards, remembering, during the race, the times one of you wanted to give up and was kept going through the other's encouragement – sometimes *forceful* encouragement! – to keep going until, finally, you crossed the line and received your medal.

I have a friend who's part of an amateur ballet company. Each year they put on a major production of a well-known ballet such as *Swan Lake* or *The Nutcracker*. The shows themselves are spectacular: the costumes, the scenery, the incredible coordination of the dancers and dances. All this couldn't be achieved without a serious commitment from those involved, from children aged three to men and women in their seventies. Hours and hours of rehearsals have to be put in to achieve the end result: a stunning two hours of glorious dance and music! And yet, only three or four performances will take place, the company being amateur. Have all those months of rehearsal been worth it to put on a mere four performances? Ask anybody in that ballet company and they'll respond with a resounding "Yes!" The reason being that the enjoyment isn't just about performing; rather, it's about being part of a *shared experience*: a shared experience which is valuable in itself, a shared experience that has a goal and produces something magical.

It seems to me there are three positives those members of the ballet company enjoy: friendship, encouragement and achievement. Running with others avails us of those same three positives. Whether we run with one other person or as part of a running club with many, we'll experience friendship: friendship that may begin because of running but may develop into something deeper; or, it may be that the friendship is already in place and a shared experience of running deepens the friendship.

I've never joined a running club – I've meant to so many times, but, as of yet, I haven't. What I have done over the years is run with other people, usually just myself and another. I started, after many years of inactivity, to run again, and, as I related earlier in the book, gave up – I ran a quarter of a mile and felt so awful I went home, put away the battered training shoes I'd had from my late teens and effectively retired from physical exercise. A friend, a keen runner, heard of my experience and persuaded me to give running another go, and I ran my first marathon with her two years later. Without her encouragement, I doubt if I'd have thought about running again.

If you run with someone else, you'll know – unless you're very disciplined – that there've been times you would have missed runs if it wasn't for your running partner. Your running partner may be the person lying next to you in bed, or he or she may live miles away, but you know that they're relying on you to run *with them*, and you're relying on them to run *with you*. If you usually meet your running partner at 6.30 a.m. at his or her house, and they live a fair distance from you, you'll know the temptation to text them and say, "Let's give it a miss today." Your running partner may even be relieved to receive your text – now you can both turn over and go back to sleep! But you both know how much better you'll feel if you do make the effort to meet and run. This shared experience of feeling good after running encourages running partners to make the effort to run, and to run at those times a solitary runner may make the choice to stay in bed!

So, having someone to run with provides us with friendship and encouragement, and it helps us achieve our running goals. Most runs will be run with a single running partner or with a small group. Once or twice a week, runs may be run with others as part of a running club. As stated above, I've never joined a running club, but I know many runners who have, and I can certainly see the advantages being a member affords. Being a member provides a great sense of camaraderie and offers many opportunities for friendship. The combined experience and expertise gleaned over many years from fellow club runners will greatly benefit new members and provide a source of encouragement. People I know who are members of running clubs say they've achieved much more as runners than they would have done had they not joined a club.

Running alone

As human beings we're instinctively social: we grow up in family units; we go to school with other pupils; we join clubs; we become team members at work; we marry and have families; and we have friends with whom we socialise.

Though so much of our time is spent with others, there are times when we need to be alone. Spending time alone is healthy. When we're alone we can think; we can reflect; we can plan. One of the best ways to spend time alone is to run by oneself.

In the New Testament we see that Jesus often spent time on his own: before beginning his public ministry, he spent forty days in the desert; before he chose his twelve disciples, he went off to be alone; after feeding the five thousand, he went up a mountain to pray, alone. Solitude was very important to him, as it should be, at times, for us.

During our solitary moments, we should also embrace silence, and in this modern age that means leaving the mobile phone switched off or out of sight. Numerous studies have found that switching off our mobile phones greatly benefits our mental health. Interestingly, there's a growing number of young people who are buying very simple phones that just make calls and send and receive texts.

In his book *Finding Sanctuary*, Abbot Christopher Jamison, a Benedictine monk, makes the point that silence and contemplation are not just the pursuits of those living in monastic communities but are practices we can all follow.[6] Running alone, without a phone in our hands and headphones in our ears, affords us opportunities for silence and contemplation. Thoughts will occur to us if we run in silence, thoughts that may not occur to us if we're listening to the news or music. God, our Father, may be trying to say something to us, and that something may be drowned out if we're distracted by the various media emanating from our phones. At first, we may experience withdrawal symptoms from being away from our phones (and that's not an exaggeration!), but if we persevere, we'll come to see the value of being "switched off" and "disconnected", even if only for a few hours a day or for the duration of a run.

As I mentioned earlier in the book, I'm fortunate to live in rural France, in a place where Nature abounds in all its glory. Roger Scruton, an English philosopher, made the point that human beings need the beauty of Nature to be fully human – we need to see it, we need to be part of it.[7] Most of us, even if we live in the most built-up areas, have access to the countryside – we may have to take a train or bus or go by car, but to experience green fields, meadows, lakes and rivers, and to gaze upon animals that inhabit these places, is to have our souls and spirits lifted. What a world God created! What human being could have designed such beauty?

To run, even if occasionally, in such environments is life-enhancing. In my time I've been a member of four gyms and have spent many hours running on treadmills, which are fine in terms of getting fit, but, to me, the treadmill was always a soulless experience: feet pounding away on a stretch of rubber whilst being bombarded with ear-splitting music wasn't, I realised, affording me the joyful experience running in fresh air brings. Treadmill running is very effective for gaining fitness, but, if you like, it's food for the body, whereas running outside in Nature – on trails, in the woods, beside a lake – is food for the soul *and* the body. The long run is especially suited to running outdoors and is so beneficial for us psychologically if done sometimes alone.

To be with others and to be alone is what it is to be a human being: we need both aspects of existence to be happy and mentally healthy. Jesus is a model for us in this way of living. As we've seen, we need, at times, to pray with others, and we, at times, need to pray alone. Running is no different: running with others and running alone is the balance we need for effective mental and physical wellbeing.

A note on yoga

Many Christians find the practice of yoga suspect; some even think it borders on the occult. However, yoga is hugely beneficial for one's fitness and mental health. As a Christian, I practise yoga "asanas" (exercises) and find that these exercises greatly aid my running. Having a flexible body is something very worthwhile, resulting in enhanced muscle strength and tone; improved respiration, energy and vitality; maintenance of a balanced metabolism; weight reduction; improved cardio and circulatory health and athletic performance; and protection from injury.

Yoga is often thought to be an easy physical practice – a great mistake! Yoga exercises and postures can be quite challenging, but they're rewarding precisely because they *are* challenging. The yoga system I practise is Ashtanga, which is quite a vigorous form of yoga. I love this way of yoga because each asana, or posture, flows into another, and the teacher only intervenes (after you've become familiar with the postures) to correct or advise. You simply turn up, unroll your mat and begin; you finish when you feel you should. If you do try Ashtanga yoga, it's very important to find a teacher qualified in this system.

Having said yoga is challenging, it's also relaxing and excellent for mental health and wellbeing. At the end of your practice, it's recommended that you spend ten or so minutes in the "corpse" posture, breathing deeply in and out, which is very calming for the mind.

So, Christians can benefit from the practice of yoga without following yoga's traditional philosophies and spiritualities. As a runner like you, I highly recommend it!

CHAPTER SIX
Finding a coach

The title of this chapter begs the question, "Do we need to be 'coached' on how to run and how to pray?" The answer must be, "No, we don't – not necessarily." A manual on running and a guidebook on prayer should provide enough information to enable us to successfully follow each discipline or practice. After all, running comes naturally to us from childhood, and prayer is simply talking and listening to God. So why would we need a coach, or guide, for either exercise?

Running coaches don't come cheap! If we employ one, what we're paying for is their knowledge and experience. This knowledge and experience can be valuable when we first take up running as a commitment to becoming fitter. A good coach can help the runner with a detailed training programme. He or she can provide the runner with realistic goals and help with planning for races. He or she can help the runner avoid injury. A coach can run alongside the runner and provide useful advice and tips. A coach can provide motivation when the runner has a dip in enthusiasm. After a number of sessions with a coach, unless one is seriously intent on achieving a very high standard of running, the runner will have taken in the knowledge the coach has imparted and will be ready to "go it alone". So, for most runners, a running coach is something temporary.

Finding someone to guide us in our spiritual exercises, a spiritual director, is more complex. The person we choose is someone to whom we may disclose much about ourselves: our thoughts, our emotions, our feelings, details about our relationships. Of course, we don't have to reveal anything personal to such a guide – we could simply ask them to help us with ways to pray, and once we've learned these methods, pray by ourselves or within a group setting.

Those who seek a spiritual director are usually seeking someone to guide them in discerning God's will for them and to help them grow closer to God in their daily life. The director will help them deepen their life of prayer, will guide them in ways of praying and help answer questions or doubts the person may have regarding their faith. How much a person reveals about themselves, their past or present situation, is up to the individual. For example, a person seeking spiritual guidance may be addicted to watching pornography on the Internet, and this addiction may be interfering with his or her relationship with God. The person may or may not choose to reveal this to a spiritual director; if he or she does reveal it, the problem has the possibility of being resolved. Another example would be a person having a deep resentment towards someone who's wronged them in the past, and this resentment is blocking their capacity to pray wholeheartedly; the director may help the person overcome this resentment and enable them to pray without constraint.

For the Christian, the point of spiritual direction is to be helped to live a life in imitation of Jesus Christ and in conformity with his teaching. Earlier in the book we talked about Søren Kierkegaard's "stages", the ultimate stage being the "religious", whereby the individual lives a life *under God's authority*. A good spiritual director can greatly help an individual arrive at this stage, whereby his or her life – actions, moral decisions, attitudes and way of thinking – is lived automatically in accordance with God's will and in conformity with Jesus' teaching.

By nature, human beings question – they seek answers and Truth. A good spiritual director will direct us towards the Truth, helping us find the answers to the questions we have. We may have questions about our faith, questions about morality, or questions about the world in which we live. He or she will help us reflect on our lives and how we're living those lives, leading us to a better understanding of who we are and how we can live better, more fulfilled lives, lives lived in conformity with God's will for us and as disciples of Jesus Christ.

The relationship we have with a spiritual director may become a close relationship: we may reveal things about ourselves we wouldn't reveal to anyone else. Finding the *right* spiritual director, therefore, is very important. If we find we don't, for whatever reason, have a rapport with a spiritual director, then we shouldn't be afraid to seek another. The spiritual journey we undertake with a director may last for years, so this rapport has to be good to be fruitful.

Usually, a spiritual director will be sought amongst those who have leadership roles in religious organisations or churches: a priest, a religious sister (nun), or a church pastor. However, spiritual direction isn't solely the preserve of religious leaders: it may be that you know someone of deep faith and wisdom, and that person may be the best person to offer you direction. What's important is that you see them fairly frequently so that a rapport can be established, thus enabling fruitful direction.

"Discernment" is a word frequently used in relation to spiritual direction, and "discernment" is an important aspect of being directed. We may not see, without help, where God is leading us; we may not be aware of what he's asking of us – a spiritual director may be able to help us understand the path God wants us to follow, helping to lead us in that direction and assisting us in making the right decision for our futures.

Of course, for the Christian, the ultimate "spiritual director" is Jesus: he is "the way, and the truth, and the life" (John 14:6). The goal of the Christian's existence is to live his or her life in imitation of Jesus – to be as Christ-like as we possibly can be – to imitate him in his compassion, in his care for people who are poor or underprivileged, in his regard for people who are elderly or disabled, in his passion for justice and in his selfless giving of his time and energy.

Where do we find the evidence for this Jesus, the life he led and the teaching he imparted? We find it chiefly in the Gospels. Though the Gospels weren't written as biographies of Jesus, they tell us what we need to know about his character and teaching, and we can grow in our imitation of him through reading them.

An important aspect of spiritual direction throughout many centuries has been *Lectio Divina*: literally, "divine reading". Lectio Divina can be practised with or without the aid of a spiritual director.

Lectio Divina consists of the following parts:

> reading a passage from the Gospels
>
> meditating on the passage
>
> praying about the passage
>
> simply resting quietly in God's presence
>
> resolving to put into practice what God has spoken to us through the passage

One can read any passage from Scripture and use it for "divine reading", but personally, I prefer to concentrate on the Gospels.

Once a Gospel passage has been chosen, it should be read at normal speed, then read again slowly. You may wish, as in the Ignatian way of prayer, to imagine yourself to be a part of the Gospel scene or as one of the characters in the Gospel passage. A particular line or something Jesus said or did may strike you.

This leads to the next part of Lectio Divina, meditation, meditating on what God may be saying to you or what he may be asking of you.

Then you may pray about what God may have said to you, asking his help if he's asking you to do something in particular.

After praying for understanding of God's message, you simply rest in God's presence: no words are necessary – just being with him is enough.

After this time of rest, we resolve to put into practice whatever teaching the Gospel passage has for us.

Lectio Divina can be practised as often as an individual desires, but perhaps once or twice a week is best. The lesson from Lectio Divina may be imparted over a few days and may need a time of reflection for it to become fully apparent. Daily reading may be overwhelming and crowd out what God may be trying to say to us.

It should be emphasised that spiritual direction is not psychotherapy; however, if a psychologist is a person of faith, and has been chosen *because* he or she is a person of faith, the two disciplines may overlap. But a person with serious psychological problems needs the help of a trained and qualified psychologist or psychiatrist before seeking spiritual direction.

CHAPTER SEVEN

Running life's course

As human beings we seem to be conditioned from the time we're born to love stories: if you want to keep a child quiet, tell him or her a good story; if you want to grab someone's attention, tell them a joke – a joke being nothing other than a small story. If you watch the soaps on TV, you're following stories about the characters' lives – the same if you read a novel.

It's amazing to think that of all the billions of people who've ever lived, no two of them have had *exactly* the same story; no two lives have had the *exact* same plot. You and I have our own unique stories. In fact, the only two things we have absolutely in common is that one day we were born and one day we'll die. God has given us free will, so what we do between those two points is largely up to us.

Of course, there are common experiences we have as we go through life: most of us will go to school; we'll be employed; we'll marry and have children; we'll grow old; and we'll experience the death of loved ones. But these common experiences are by no means certain – for instance, some of us may choose not to marry and have children. The choice is ours.

Those of us who've run races are familiar with mile or kilometre markers, telling us how far we've run and how far we've yet to run to the finish line. Those common experiences, outlined above, are like the markers in a race. They plot the course of our lives:

Mile 1: birth; Mile 2: school; Mile 3: first employment; Mile 4: serious girlfriend or boyfriend; Mile 5: marriage; Mile 6: first child; Mile 7: first grandchild; Mile 8: death of a parent; Mile 9: retirement; Mile 10: death.

Those ten markers may vary, but they're common to a large proportion of humanity. Yet, still, the only *absolute* common factors we all share are birth and death. In running terms, we could compare running a race to living a life: we set off at the start, and we end at the finishing line. How we run the race is entirely up to us.

Countless people before us have run the same races we've run or plan to run; countless people before us have lived the lives we're now living. Wouldn't it make sense, then, to learn from their experience? What were the mistakes they made? What were the successes they achieved, and how did they achieve them?

We hear so much these days about "role models", a role model being someone who's supposed to be a great example of how others should live. Very often people are criticised for not being the role models they're supposed to be; for instance, the footballer who cheats on the pitch is a bad example to young people, or the religious leader caught having an affair is a bad example to his congregation. Human beings are flawed, and no human being can be the perfect role model. The positive aspect of a role model's flaws is that we can learn from their mistakes as well as from their virtues.

Each religious tradition has had founders and adherents who've lived exemplary lives – men and women who inspire those who follow them and adhere to the traditions they began. We may think of the Buddha, Muhammad, Moses, Jesus and so on. In the Christian tradition we also have the examples of the saints: St Paul, St Augustine, St Francis of Assisi, St Bernadette, St Theresa and many more. Often, saints were flawed individuals who had their lives transformed when they accepted Jesus as God's Son and then lived their lives in conformity with his teaching. This can be true for us: each of us has flaws, but if we truly embrace Jesus as God's Son, and live by his teaching, we can be transformed into the people we were created to be.

I remember waiting to see my doctor once. On a table, in the surgery waiting room, were various magazines. From a choice of *Woman's Realm*, *Woman's Own* and *Hello!*, I chose *Hello!* Leafing through the magazine the thought occurred to me, "Why do people want to look at page after page of glossy photographs, photographs picturing people with enough money to buy very expensive designer clothes and live in palatial houses?" And the only answer I could think of was that the magazine, and others like it, tap into our fantasies – for twenty minutes you can imagine yourself being that famous actor living in that mansion in the leafy suburbs, with nothing much to do except plan your next exotic holiday. But then you put the magazine down, and you have to become yourself again. But being yourself is far better because "yourself" is the person God created.

God created us to be saints! But what is a saint, and how do we achieve sainthood? Saints are people who show a certain holiness throughout their lives, and they become saintly by being themselves. But what do we mean by "being themselves"? When God created us, he created us as saintly beings: people with a capacity to do the right thing on every occasion and in every circumstance. So, our true character, our *real* character, is to be saintly. But we're also prone to do wrong, to sin, and it's when we sin that we're *not* truly ourselves: we're going *against* the nature God created us with, which is perhaps why the sinful things we do never really make us happy, because we're acting *contrary* to our true selves, and happiness only ultimately comes from being genuinely who we are.

I don't suppose many of us think of ourselves as "holy", as candidates for sainthood. We might think we're OK: we try to get on with people and wouldn't do them any harm, but acting like saints seems beyond us most of the time. But we *are* saintly because we're people God created in his own image. So, holiness and saintliness aren't virtues we have to work at, to strive after, but rather something we have to *display*: those virtues are there within us already – they're inherent facets of our nature, that is, our *true* nature.

We all know people who are saints: people in our own families or people we work with. What makes them saints is being the people they are and living the lives God created them to live.

When we meet God, he won't say to us, "Did you become like those rich people in the glossy magazines?" He won't even ask us if we became like Mother Teresa or St Francis of Assisi. But he might ask us, "Did you become the person I intended you to be?" God created us to be saintly, and the best way to be a saint is to be ourselves – that is, to be our *true selves*.

There are many "role models" we could choose to follow; there are many examples of great people who've lived or are living exemplary lives. We may wish to emulate the virtues of a politician, a philanthropist, an athlete, an author, a religious leader or someone we know personally. We all have our own heroes or heroines, people who inspire us to live good lives or to do great things.

For Christians, the greatest exemplar we have is Jesus. No other person in history has had the impact on the world he's had and still has. Author Henry G. Bosch has made this observation:

> *Socrates taught for forty years, Plato for fifty, Aristotle for forty, and Jesus for only three. Yet the influence of Christ's three-year ministry infinitely transcends the impact left by the combined hundred and thirty years of teaching from these men who are among the greatest philosophers of all antiquity. Jesus painted no pictures, yet some of the finest paintings of Raphael, Michelangelo and Leonardo da Vinci received their inspiration from him. Jesus wrote no poetry, but Dante, Milton, and scores of the world's greatest poets were inspired by him. Jesus composed no music, still Haydn, Handel, Beethoven, Bach and Mendelssohn reached their highest perfection of melody in the hymns, symphonies, and oratorios they composed in his praise. Every sphere of human greatness has been enriched by this humble carpenter of Nazareth.*[8]

No other historical figure, like Jesus, has inspired human beings to live their lives so selflessly for the good of others. His teachings, through the accounts of the New Testament, are widely known today. His parables and sayings continue to inform our moral thinking and language. We even mark time from before he was born to the years after he was born – this we do when we talk in terms of BC and AD. Jesus championed the "rights" of the oppressed long before any country or bill enacted them: he treated women as equals; he taught us that human rights are intrinsic to every human being, no matter what their race or skin colour; he instructed us to give humanitarian aid wherever that aid is needed. He gave us the overarching "Golden Rule": "In everything do to others as you would have them do to you" (Matthew 7:12).

What better "role model" than Jesus could we have to base our lives on? What better exemplar could we strive to imitate?

When we run a race, we follow a predetermined course – if we deviate from that course, we'll be disqualified. Like a race, life is a predetermined course in the sense that we're born and we'll die, but unlike a race, we can choose our own route between these two points. Life is infinitely more complicated than running a race – we can get through a race without much assistance – but life, being so much more complicated, is greatly helped if we have a guide.

The obvious guide for the Christian is Jesus. Here's someone who's already run life's course, someone who's lived the gamut of human emotions and experiences, someone who even suffered brutal execution, but through it all he remained compassionate and forgiving and steadfast in the trust he placed in his Father.

But, you may say, Jesus is God's Son – surely he wasn't *fully* human in the sense that we are? But he was and is – every emotion we experience was experienced by Jesus when he was amongst us: joys, sorrows, heartaches, disappointments, love, sympathy, physical pain, doubts, friendship. Every emotion or feeling that's a part of human existence was felt by Jesus. So he knows all aspects of what we go through: he can empathise with us when we're struggling; he can rejoice with us when life is good; he can mourn with us when we suffer a bereavement; he can celebrate life with us when we hold a newly born infant or watch children playing; he can understand our times of doubt; like us, in moments of despair, he knows what it is to wonder if God has abandoned him; he knows what we experience when we're facing the end of our lives, and the pain we may be suffering as we approach death; and he knows, like us, what it is to have faith and the hope of eternal life.

We know a lot, then, about Jesus: through the Gospels we have insights into his character, his way of thinking, his views on different matters. Is he, therefore, the one we want as our chief guide in life? If he is, what will his guidance bring us? How will our lives be different if we accept his guidance?

Before we can be guided by Jesus, a few preliminaries are required: firstly, we have to ask him for his guidance and then place our trust in him and the guidance he offers us. Having done so, what will be different about our lives? The following list delineates a few of those differences:

We'll be less anxious about matters that concern us.

We'll be more patient and understanding of others.

We'll have more compassion for those who suffer.

We'll have a deepened sense of what is just and right.

We'll have a real sense of joy and contentment.

We'll be more generous with our time and resources.

We'll find it easier to resist temptation.

We'll find life has more colour and zest.

We'll feel happier and more fulfilled.

We'll know a real sense of freedom.

Every time we lace up our running shoes, we have a goal. The goal may be simply to blow off some cobwebs and enjoy the fresh air. It may be another run on the road to a certain level of fitness. It may be another run in preparation for an upcoming race. Each time we enter a race, we also have a goal – to finish the race in the best time we can.

Though we may not be conscious of it, during each run and each race, we have another goal: to avoid injury. Almost without thinking, before we run, we may stretch and then stretch again after the run. Our aim is to finish a run without injury and to reach our destination – the end of a training run or the race's finishing line – as physically unaffected as possible, with no pulled muscles or hamstrings: we want to arrive at the end of a run safely!

Unfortunately, unless extremely lucky, runners will sustain an injury at some point, often despite all precautions to avoid physical setbacks. The severity of an injury can be reduced if appropriate exercises are done prior to running, and the time it takes for an injury to heal may be shortened if we have a good stretching regime in place as part of our general fitness programme.

Life, like running, will inflict injuries on us: they may be physical injuries or psychological injuries – some may be avoidable, others inevitable. A healthy lifestyle may help us avoid heart disease; if we're genetically prone to cancer, we may not be able to escape its consequences. We may be good husbands or wives, doing all we can to forge successful marriages; we may suffer immense heartache if our partners leave us for somebody else. We all want to live as happily as possible, and to a large extent, happiness lies in the choices and decisions we make. Likewise, *un*-happiness also lies in the choices and decisions we make.

Jesus tells us, "I came that they may have life, and have it abundantly" (John 10:10); he also tells us he is the "way" – the "way" to this abundant life, therefore, is through Jesus. We can follow our own path, or we can follow his. Again, this is our choice to make. Whilst it's not inevitable that *not* choosing Jesus' path will lead to unhappiness – after all, there are millions of people who never give Jesus or God a second thought, and they seem to be living happy lives – making the choice to follow his way can help us avoid much heartache and disappointment as we go through life. How is this so?

If you re-read those ten points listed above, outlining the difference following Jesus makes, you'll see that they offer us peace, freedom and hope. We have *peace* because we know we're not alone: God is with us and Jesus is guiding us. We have peace because we're less anxious, knowing that our cares and worries can be placed in God's hands, and he'll share the burden with us. We have peace because we see others as God's sons and daughters, and in doing so, we have more tolerance and patience for them; thus, they become less irritating and threatening. We have *freedom* from sin when we choose Jesus' way and not our own and freedom from the heartache that sin often brings. We have the freedom of not following the herd when the herd is wrong or is going in the wrong direction. We have the freedom to be ourselves, the people God created, and not be concerned with what others think of us. We have *hope* for the future, knowing that despite the world's and our own troubles, God will make all things right. We have hope when so much that's happening in the world seems to be doom and gloom, the hope of knowing God is ultimately in control. We have the hope of knowing that this life isn't all there is – we have the hope of an eternal life to come.

You may remember a few years ago it was fashionable for some Christians to wear wristbands with "WWJD?" imprinted on them. WWJD? stood for "What Would Jesus Do?" The idea was that when faced with a moral or ethical decision, the wearer would glance at the wristband and ask him- or herself that question, reflect on it, and then make a decision based on what he or she imagined Jesus doing in the same circumstance.

The trend for wristbands espousing various causes seems to have gone out of fashion, but the "WWJD?" question is a useful one, one we could ask ourselves when faced with a situation demanding a moral decision. If we look at three scenarios, it may help us to understand the usefulness of such a question.

Scenario One: You come home from work tired, and all you want to do is eat and have a relaxing evening. However, an elderly relative is in hospital and could really do with a visit. You ask yourself the question, "What would Jesus do?"

Scenario Two: A friend has asked you over to his house for a BBQ and has let you know that someone you're very attracted to will be there. You know this someone is also attracted to you, and he or she has hinted in the past that they would welcome a physical relationship with you. However, you know this person is married. You ask yourself the question, "What would Jesus do?"

Scenario Three: Your company supplies you with a credit card to be used to fill up your company car with petrol. The proprietor of the petrol station tells you he has no objection if you purchase some groceries on the card, as well as petrol, but only petrol will be shown on the credit card statement. You ask yourself the question, "What would Jesus do?"

These scenarios and questions demonstrate that following Jesus isn't some vague, nebulous, feel-good pastime; rather it requires a willingness to live by his standards, doing our best to imitate his actions and attitudes. St Paul urges us to "put on the Lord Jesus Christ" (Romans 13:14) and "let the same mind be in [us] that was in Christ Jesus" (Philippians 2:5). In other words, we are to have a Christ-like mindset, and from this mindset will flow Christ-like thinking and actions.

The most obvious way to understand the mind of Christ is to study how he lived and thought, and our best source for this understanding is the Gospels. As stated earlier, the Gospels weren't written as biographies of Jesus – we know very little about his life between his birth and the start of his public ministry. Rather, they were written to help us understand his nature – that he is fully human and fully divine – and to convey to us his teaching.

As well as the Gospels themselves, we can also learn much about Jesus' thinking and teaching with the aid of a good "commentary". In this respect I would recommend William Barclay's series of Gospel commentaries and also Fulton J. Sheen's *The Life of Christ*. Both authors provide deep insights into Jesus' life and teaching, and the commentaries are vividly written. Spiritual reading has an important role to play in our spiritual lives, whether the writing is directly concerned with the life of Jesus or other aspects of our faith. If possible, spiritual reading should be a part of our daily life.

As runners and as people of faith, we're completing life's course together. You may be on lap two, aged twenty-something; you may be in your forties, on lap three; or in your sixties, on lap five; or in your seventies or eighties on the last lap. One thing's for sure: the course of life goes very quickly! Doubtless those on the last lap will remember very clearly being on lap two, then speeding through laps three, four and five. Countless millions have run life's course before us and are now with God. You may be in the USA, China, Italy, Nigeria, Peru, Afghanistan or another country, but we share two wonderful things in common: we're runners and we're people of faith, and, as such, we're completing life's course *together*. No matter which particular lap we happen to be on at this moment, we all share a common goal: eternal life in God's heavenly Kingdom. At the end of our lives, may we say with St Paul:

> *I have fought the good fight,*
> *I have finished the race,*
> *I have kept the faith.*
>   *(2 Timothy 4:7)*

CHAPTER EIGHT

The challenge of the marathon

According to a 2019 report from the International Institute for Race Medicine, 1.1 million people complete a marathon each year, which is roughly 0.014 per cent of the world's population.[9] That statistic shows that those who've completed running those gruelling 26.2 miles belong to a fairly exclusive club. Those figures may also demonstrate that the rest of the world's population has more sense! After all, why would you want to put yourself through sixteen to twenty-four weeks of hard, time-consuming training and then the energy-draining, leg-muscle-sapping twenty-six miles of the marathon itself? Quite simply, because it's one of life's great achievements! Not many of us will have a hit record or write a best-selling novel or share a pitch with Lionel Messi, but if you're reasonably fit and run regularly, you can run a marathon!

A marathon may not be the ultimate test for a runner – there are those who run over a hundred miles through deserts! – but a test it is, nonetheless, and a very real test of dedication, discipline and endurance. I remember thinking – it must have been after sixteen or seventeen miles into my first marathon – "If I can finish this, I can do anything." That feeling has stayed with me: when faced with a difficult situation, that particular marathon comes to mind, and I remember those last punishing miles and the times I just wanted to stop, hobble to the side of the course and sit down, not caring if I never ran again. What kept me going was sheer willpower and asking for God's help, telling myself to just get through another half-mile, then another half-mile – then another half-mile, until the finishing line loomed like a vision of heaven. I'm sure all who've completed marathons would agree that we have depths within us we never imagined; we have a resilience we only find when life is at its toughest. Look at those who care at home for a husband or wife with dementia or those whose child is born with a disability – the love and care people show in these and similar situations is wonderful to behold: they find a spirit and strength they probably didn't realise they possessed.

Running a marathon is not only a physical challenge but also a mental one. You should be running a minimum of twenty miles per week before you begin a sixteen- to twenty-four-week marathon training programme, with preferably a few 10K's under your belt.

If you *are* running those twenty miles per week, you already have a certain physical and mental discipline – twenty miles may not seem much, but you still have to get yourself out of the door in all weathers, perhaps very early in the morning before work, and run. However, the training for a marathon covers many weeks and many runs, runs of varying distances of up to twenty-two miles. Needless to say, those weeks of high mileage as they escalate will be physically taxing. As the mileage increases, it will become more mentally taxing, and this is where discipline and commitment are essential. When you have a twelve-mile training run to complete on an early, wet Thursday morning, possibly before work, that requires commitment! When you come home from work after a tiring day and it's dark outside, and you have a fifteen-mile training run to go on, that requires discipline! It's not only running the marathon itself that instils resilience and character, but those many weeks of consistent choices: choices made to leave the house and run.

If your marathon training is done alone, you'll probably need even more discipline to get you through those long weeks. I've run two marathons alone – alone, both during the training and the actual marathons – and I can testify that the training and the marathon are easier if you have a running partner. But, if you complete the training alone, you won't feel lonely when you run the marathon: you may not know anyone running alongside you, but you'll interact with quite a few people over the course of those twenty-six miles, and the sheer exhilaration of running with thousands of others will lift your heart and spur you on.

Being in this part of France, I'm very fortunate to be living on the route to a famous and ancient pilgrimage destination: Compostela, in Northern Spain. The pilgrimage is known as the "Camino de Santiago" or "The Way of St James". Pilgrims have walked this "Way" since the tenth century, after the relics of St James the Great, one of Jesus' twelve disciples, were discovered near the town of Compostela.

When pilgrims arrive at Compostela, they go to the cathedral armed with their books of *credencials* – credencials are the stamps that are entered into the books as proof they've completed the walk. Upon presentation of the completed books, the pilgrims are awarded their certificates, stating the walk has been successfully accomplished.

Not far from where I live, on this route, is a bar, and pilgrims go to this bar to have one of the credencials stamped into their books, as they do in other accredited bars and churches along the way. This has given me the opportunity to talk to many pilgrims – pilgrims from all over the world. It's always fascinating to hear their motives for walking up to a thousand miles to Compostela. In my experience, 50 per cent of pilgrims walk for religious reasons and 50 per cent for other, non-religious, reasons. Though the fundamental motivations for making the pilgrimage may differ – some for religious reasons, others not – they overlap in many cases. High on the list of reasons for the religious pilgrim is thanksgiving: thanking God for perhaps the birth of a child or a successful outcome after an operation. The religious person may also walk as an act of penance for some misdemeanour of the past (this was very often the case with pilgrims in previous centuries). High on both the religious and non-religious persons' reasons is walking in memory of a loved one who's died.

The idea of "pilgrimage" is very ancient and is still popular today: Christians flock each year to the shrines of Our Lady of Lourdes in France, Guadalupe in Mexico, Knock in Ireland and to the Holy Land in Israel, the place of Jesus' birth, life and death; Muslims make the pilgrimage, or Hajj, to Mecca in Saudi Arabia; other faiths have their own places of pilgrimage.

The reasons people run marathons echo the reasons people make pilgrimages. A common sight on the running vests of those running a marathon will be pictures of loved ones, over which are written words such as, "in memory of Mum" or "in memory of Dad". A large percentage of runners will be running for a charity that's close to their hearts. Like those who make pilgrimages to religious sites, runners run marathons more often than not *for a reason*, whether this reason is openly stated or is kept silently in the runner's mind and heart.

A runner who has a religious faith, then, can run a marathon for the same reasons religious people make a pilgrimage: it could be in thanksgiving to God for a specific reason; it could be for the repose of the soul of a loved one who's died; it could be to ask God's blessing on a new venture; it could be a way of repenting a past sin; it could be to ask God's help in overcoming an addiction. To run a marathon for one of these reasons, or a similar reason, provides the runner with a *purpose* to run, and this purpose will help carry him or her through the weeks and months of training and over the course of the marathon's twenty-six miles.

Often, we hear the phrases, "God will test us" or "God is testing me." I'm not sure God "tests" us in the sense that these phrases are often meant – that God deliberately chooses to inflict, say, an illness on us, or some other misfortune, as was the case with Job in the Old Testament. How are we meant to pass the test, and what constitutes a pass? Rather, I think God will *challenge* us. He may ask us to do something we may not want to do; he may ask us to take on a task we don't feel we're up to; he may challenge us to go the extra mile in something we're doing already. A sign that the challenge is genuinely from God is that it will be for the good of others – it won't be a challenge for a challenge's sake, just to see if we can rise to it.

If God does challenge us, we can be certain he'll provide us with the wherewithal to meet the challenge – he won't ask us to do anything we're not capable of doing.

If we want an example of someone who didn't feel up to the task God was asking him to fulfil, we may look no further than St Peter. Peter, a simple fisherman, was asked by Jesus to be the "rock" upon which he'd build his Church. Saints Peter and Paul are known as the "pillars of the Church" and Jesus harnessed their different characters to become the Church's firm foundation. On the face of it, Paul would have been a more obvious choice to lead the fledgling group of Christians: a dynamic individual who did everything with the utmost enthusiasm. Before his famous conversion, he persecuted Christians, and he did it with a vengeance; if he was acting as Christ's apostle, he did it fearlessly. As a trained rabbi, Paul was steeped in the minutiae of Jewish Law; he was a man of great intellect. Why did Jesus, then, choose Peter to carry out such a crucial role? We can only surmise that Jesus knew that this simple fisherman had in him the necessary capacity for leadership. Jesus saw in Peter qualities Peter couldn't see in himself. If God asks something of us, the same applies: we have the necessary qualities to make God's plans come to fruition, even if those qualities don't seem obvious to us.

The decision to run a marathon is, at first, exhilarating – after the initial feeling of excitement and enthusiasm, the prospect of months of training and running twenty-six miles can be daunting. At this point, you don't know if you can do it, but you trust yourself, accept the challenge and resolve to do your best. It's similar with a challenge from God: we're not sure if we can succeed in fulfilling the challenge. What's needed is trust – trust that God wouldn't ask us to do something for which we haven't the capacity. If we accept God's challenge, he'll provide us with what's necessary for us to meet it successfully. All God asks is that we do our best, assured that he's with us in what we do.

If you take up the challenge of the marathon, you won't regret it, and, hopefully, you'll find those latent depths and strengths you may not realise you have, enabling you to become more confident and resilient afterwards. If God asks something of you, you won't regret responding positively to his request. You have your own qualities to draw on, and you have God's help – and that's a powerful combination!

CHAPTER NINE
Using time effectively

St Alphonsus Liguori, the founder of the Redemptorist religious order, made a vow never to waste a second. Whether Alphonsus managed to keep that vow, we don't know, but he must have been superhuman if he did!

We might ask Alphonsus what he considered "waste" in terms of time. Is staring out of the window wasted time? Is watching TV wasted time? Is going for a Sunday afternoon drive in the countryside wasted time? Well, of course not! And if we aren't engaged in those activities, what things would we be doing that qualify as "productive time"?

Perhaps it would be more helpful if we categorised time as "nourishing time" and "unhealthy time". Of course, these categories are subjective: what I consider "nourishing time", you may consider a waste of time; similarly, what I consider "unhealthy time" you may think of as enjoyable time. However, these categories become less subjective when we view them from the perspective of our faith, as then we can apply an objective standard – God's standard – by which to judge whether we're spending time in a particular way *nourishingly* or *unhealthily*.

There are countless books and videos on the subject of "time management", advising how, through the best use of time, to make each day as productive as possible. This advice usually refers to work-based activity, and the advice given can be very valuable. But what about the time we have away from the workplace? Does this time have to be "managed" to such an extent? Of course, certain tasks during the day are mandatory: cooking for the children, cleaning the house, paying the bills and so on. We're then left with the time we have solely for ourselves, time we call "leisure". How are we spending these hours of leisure? Are we filling them with content that's nourishing or content that leaves us dispirited?

A few years ago, I joined Facebook, and it was good to see what people I knew were up to. I became a member of a few groups and gleaned useful information about events happening in my area. However, I found myself in bed at night, not reaching for a book, but picking up the phone and scrolling through endless clips of animals doing amusing things, people engaged in road-rage incidents and even brutal street fights. This became addictive, and each time I put the phone down, I felt dejected and empty. Not only had I wasted time – time I could have spent reading a book – but I was demoralised: I knew I was bombarding my mind with trash, with content that was utterly devoid of anything wholesome or nutritional. Looking at these clips was not conducive to sleep and left me in a state of restlessness. I've never "been on" Twitter, or X, as it's now called, but I understand them to be on par with Facebook for consuming huge amounts of their subscribers' time. I resolved to unsubscribe from Facebook and renew the great pleasure reading books affords us.

Facebook is one example whereby, if we're not careful, we can spend hours a day filling our time with unhealthy content. The addictive nature of platforms such as Facebook can't be overestimated, and it can be very difficult to break the Facebook habit. We live in an age of information technology and, unless we become hermits, it's very difficult not to be a part of this digital world.

Can it be a coincidence that, as technology increases, religiosity decreases? This appears to be the case in the Western world – the world where this technology is most affordable. As people of faith, we have to live with, and use, this technology, but treat it with caution. We weren't created to spend hours staring at screens, and studies are showing just how detrimental to our wellbeing screen addiction has become. The answer to this problem is obvious: we have to ration the time we spend on social media. Those of us who can remember when the only telephone we had was on the hallway table have to relearn what it is not to constantly reach for a device which can rob us of so much time, time we could be filling with healthier content.

The above may seem overcritical of social media and the chief gateway to such media, the mobile phone. However, social media can be used for good purposes, and the mobile phone is a wondrous device to behold. How we use such content and technology is of crucial importance: when we use them, are they nutritionally beneficial or unhealthily detrimental for us, mentally and spiritually?

Time spent on social media will usually be part of our leisure time. How do we best fill the rest of the time we have to ourselves? To spend time healthily and productively, we need to separate our leisure time into four segments: time for God, time for ourselves, time for friends and family, and time for exercise.

Time for God

Previous pages in this book have illustrated the importance of prayer: that we talk to and listen to God our Father and to his Son, Jesus. A relationship without communication is a relationship that doesn't exist. The more communicative the relationship, the deeper the relationship becomes. To arrive at a point of intimacy in a relationship requires frequent communication, opening ourselves to another and allowing them to reveal themselves to us. Relationships, if they're to flourish, require time, and this time has to be "made", to be "set aside". A relationship based on "when I can fit it in" or "when I feel up to it" is a poor relationship and one that's unlikely to last.

If our aim is to have an intimate relationship with God and to enjoy the benefits such a relationship brings, spending time with God is essential, and this time has to be found each day. The ways we spend time with God may vary: we can be with him as we pray set prayers; we can be with him in silence; we can be with him as we read a passage of Scripture; we can be with him as we perform a task done in his name. Time spent with God is never wasted, and we invariably come away from our time with him refreshed and spiritually nourished.

Time for ourselves

The time we spend doing the things we like to do is time very well spent and helps us to be balanced people. This time may be spent pursuing a hobby, reading, going for a walk, watching a film or having a long bath. Whatever it is we find enjoyable is beneficial for our mental health and shouldn't induce in us any sense of guilt – guilt because we're not doing something with or for others. Doing the things we like to do makes us happy, and if we're happy, our relationships and our own sense of wellbeing can only benefit.

Time for friends and family

Some of us seem to have a gift for establishing, nurturing and sustaining friendships; some of us are less adept at doing so. Those who have this gift are, according to psychologists and medics, the fortunate ones: mental and physical health are greatly enhanced if we have close friends and we communicate with them regularly. A good, true friend is somebody you can trust, on whom you can rely, to whom you can be open and honest about yourself. To have such a friend is to be blessed. Friendship, like any relationship, can wither from neglect and, therefore, has to be afforded time if it is to flourish and be lasting. Friendships can be deep even if two friends live in different countries, but these friendships will have been forged through personal encounters: from being physically present to each other in the past. Texting is no adequate substitute for meeting face-to-face; rather, healthy friendships require friends to meet physically. Those of us who pay less attention to our friendships than we should would do well to remind ourselves how precious a gift friendship is and perhaps resolve to give them the time and effort they deserve. We can only gain from doing so, mentally and physically.

The old saying, "You can choose your friends, but not your family," is obviously true. Most of us are fortunate to be born into and to be raised in loving and supportive families; others are not so fortunate and experience varying degrees of familial dysfunction, whether that be mental or sexual abuse, alcoholism, drug misuse or poverty due to financial mismanagement. The families we grow up in have a profound effect on our psychology, our outlook and our future prospects in life. Stable family life, therefore, is crucial for the wellbeing of the individual and for the good of the societies in which we live.

If we *are* fortunate to have experienced a stable family background, and that positive experience continues into adult life, it makes sense to foster and develop family relationships as best, and for as long as, we can.

Again, communication is the key to sustaining good relationships. Talking regularly, preferably face-to-face, with members of our families is beneficial for us in many ways, reminding us of who we are and where we came from, reinforcing the morals and values instilled in us from childhood and knowing we'll have support when we need it from those who care for us most.

When we reach adulthood it's natural for us to move away from home and become caught up in our own concerns and pursuits, and it's very easy for weeks, perhaps months, to slip by without us talking to our parents or siblings. To avoid this "drift", a resolution to keep in touch is important: a resolution to make the time to be with, or at least to communicate regularly with, family members.

Time for exercise

I remember meeting someone I knew as I came to the end of a morning run, and this person jokingly remarked, "People like you want to live for ever. The bad news is – when your time's up, it's up!"

I thought about this remark throughout the day, and it occurred to me that, no, I certainly don't want to live for ever, but whilst I'm alive I want to be as healthy as I can be and able to perform physical tasks free from discomfort and pain for as long as possible. I then thought, "Being able to do physical tasks without pain is a demonstrable, visible proof of fitness, but what about the hidden, invisible benefits?" I have a friend, a doctor, who pointed out the *unseen* reasons to exercise, amongst which are that it:

improves memory and brain function (in all age groups)

protects against chronic diseases

aids in weight management

lowers blood pressure and improves heart health

improves quality of sleep

reduces feelings of anxiety and depression

improves mood and sense of wellbeing

can add years to one's lifespan

The question then becomes, why *not* exercise? An answer to this question may be that physical exercise can make our bodies feel uncomfortable. Then the issue becomes a cost–benefit analysis: is the bodily discomfort worthwhile if the health benefits exercising brings are so great? As runners, we obviously believe it is worthwhile, and, being worthwhile, worth finding the time to exercise.

If we find the time to make these four points a part of our daily life, or to at least engage in them on a regular basis, life should prove to be healthier and more enjoyable. The following quote from H. Jackson Brown is worth pondering:

> *Please don't say you haven't enough time. You have exactly the same number of hours per day as Michelangelo, Mother Teresa, Louis Pasteur, Leonardo da Vinci and Albert Einstein.*[10]

For what's important to us, it's time to make the time!

CONCLUSION

If you've read this book thus far, it's likely you're a runner and a person of faith. Less likely, but possible, is that you've read the book thus far and would like to be a runner or a person of faith – or both!

My hope is that what you've read has inspired you to deepen your faith and remain committed to running. Or to discover the joy having a faith brings and come to realise the benefits of becoming a runner. Even if you only begin one of these practices – a relationship with God or becoming a runner – this book will have been worth writing and worth reading.

I write these concluding words at a time of global instability: a post-pandemic world and a world, due to Russia's invasion of Ukraine, of economic uncertainty; a world in which the poorest are still the poorest, and even those middle-earners who've hitherto not known hardship are struggling financially.

History teaches us that the world has always undergone turbulent times, often more turbulent and traumatic than our own, and, in all likelihood, will go on experiencing harrowing periods in future – such is the capacity of some human beings to pursue wealth and power to the detriment of the majority, following their own paths and not God's.

And yet, the world always has been, and always will be, a good world simply because God created it. Jesus Christ, God's Son, came into the world and sanctified it with his presence, inspiring billions of people to live as he lived and ensure the world remains a world in which good will always triumph over evil. In the hearts of the vast majority of human beings, there is more good than bad, and therein lies the hope for today and for the future.

Each of us, living our faith as best we can, plays a small but significant part in making the world the good world it is. We'll inhabit this world for a certain number of years – perhaps few, perhaps many – what's important is that we enjoy it whilst we're here, be the people God wants us to be, and pass on as good a world as we can to the next generation.

> *Do not let your hearts be troubled. Believe in God, believe also in me.*
> *(John 14:1)*

ACKNOWLEDGEMENTS

I would like to thank my parents, Mary and John, for giving me the gift of faith and showing me how to live that faith. May they rest in peace.

My thanks go to Fiona Sweeney for encouraging me to begin running again and for the years, and the marathon, we ran together.

I offer a special thanks to my present running partner, Catriona MacLeay, for the many, many runs we've run together and for the runs yet to come!

Finally, my thanks to Krista Nelson for her patient editing and helpful suggestions.

St Dizier Masbaraud, France
August, 2023

ABOUT THE AUTHOR

James, this book's author, conducts running and walking retreats in the beautiful French countryside near Limoges. Accommodation is at the wonderful Maison Les Berry's guest house, Bourganeuf, with all food freshly home-made. For further information, please email James at jamesmcshane1234@aol.com.

I was born in Liverpool and am a Catholic priest of Brentwood Diocese, United Kingdom. From my earliest days, I've always been a runner, representing my school in cross-country events. I've completed three London marathons and countless half-marathons and 10K runs.

I began giving retreats on "Running and Spirituality" in my diocese after becoming fascinated by the body's and mind's (soul's) complementary natures and how these aspects of our being, when healthy, enhance our physical and spiritual wellbeing and sense of worth.

I can't imagine life without running, and I can't imagine life without praying. I give God thanks that most days I can do both!

James McShane

ENDNOTES

1   When I was running the 2002 London Marathon, Haile Gebrselassie was the guest speaker and made this comment during his speech.

2   Saint Augustine of Hippo, *Confessions*, book 1, chapter 1.

3   Martin Luther King Jr, "I Have a Dream," August 28, 1963, Lincoln Memorial, Washington DC, Transcript, NPR.org, https://www.npr.org/2010/01/18/122701268/i-have-a-dream-speech-in-its-entirety

4   Søren Kierkegaard, *Either/Or: A Fragment of Life* (Penguin Classics, 1992).

5   Saint Augustine of Hippo, Sermon 227, "Preached on the Holy Day of Easter to the Infantes, on the Sacraments," in *The Works of Saint Augustine: A Translation for the 21st Century*, part 3, volume 6, Sermons, trans. Edmund Hill (New City Press, 1993).

6   Christopher Jamison, *Finding Sanctuary: Monastic Steps for Everyday Life* (Weidenfeld & Nicolson, 2010).

7   Roger Scruton, *Beauty* (Oxford University Press, 2009).

8   Dr M.R. DeHaan and Henry Bosch, *Our Daily Bread* (Zondervan, 1959).

9   *The State of Running 2019*, The International Institute for Race Medicine, https://racemedicine.org/the-state-of-running-2019/

10 H. Jackson Brown, *Life's Little Instruction Book: 511 Suggestions, Observations, and Reminders on How to Live a Happy and Rewarding Life* (Rutledge Hill Press, 2000).